brand new brand thinking

brand new brand thinking

brought to life by 11 experts who do

edited by merry baskin and mark earls

**KOGAN
PAGE**

London and Sterling, VA

First published in Great Britain and the United States by Kogan Page Limited in 2002.
Reprinted in 2003 (twice)

120 Pentonville Road
London N1 9JN
United Kingdom
www.kogan-page.co.uk

22883 Quicksilver Drive
Sterling VA 20116-2012
USA

British Library Cataloguing in Publication Data

A CIP record for this book is available from the British Library

ISBN 0 7494 3678 6

Typeset by Saxon Graphics Ltd, Derby
Printed and bound in Great Britain by Biddles Ltd, *www.biddles.co.uk*

Contents

Foreword

Dominic Mills
Editorial Director, Campaign

Being invited to write the foreword to this Account Planning Group book on brand thinking is rather like being a sports writer who, by some amazing chain of events, finds himself coming off the bench for Manchester United in a crucial premiership match: it's very nice, but what I am doing here on the same pitch as my heroes?

I've never worked in advertising, I've never worked for a client, and I can't foresee the circumstances in which I would. On the other hand, like the dedicated sports reporter, I've had one of the best seats in the stadium for the last decade. I've seen the agony; I've seen the ecstasy; I've seen the blood, sweat and tears. I dare say, through my time editing and writing for *Campaign*, I've been the cause of some of those emotions.

One of the things I love about the advertising business is its passion. The passion with which it goes about its work; and the passion with which it argues with itself about this theory or that, this methodology or that, this ad or that ad, and this or that strategy. Everybody knows, of course, that there is no single right answer or theory (although there are plenty of wrong ones), but for all that uncertainty the passion remains.

That's why this book matters. You don't have to agree with everything it says to gain from it. You may even violently disagree with some of its assertions – I did – but it'll make you think. Even if those ideas, all of them articulated with passion and a clarity of thought, make you just think for a nano-second about your own beliefs, then that is a job well done.

Can it really be, for example, as Adam Stagliano amd Damian O'Malley claim, that the best brands are built from the inside out by ignoring consumers? Well, that certainly challenges a lot of assumptions. And what about the assertion by Colin Mitchell that we are moving into the era of the corporate brand? And this in an era of the Ford tyre debacle, Enron and Andersen.

If you think, however, that this is a collection of essays by youthful rebels seeking only to provoke, reconsider. I hesitate to do the maths, but if you add up the collective advertising and branding experience of the authors here it comes to more than 300 years. Better still, they're from a collection of different markets and different cultures. That's a lot of collective wisdom and knowledge distilled in an accessible form from a variety of perspectives. Read any chapter and you will find something there that helps your understanding of the alchemy that is advertising and branding or makes you reassess your own views.

We all need to remember too that this book is published against a background of unprecedented upheaval and uncertainty for those in our business. There are fundamental structural issues to address, big media debates to be had and a myriad of those agonized 'whither advertising?' questions to worry away at. None of the chapters in this book sets out to answer those questions specifically, but along the way they cast much illumination.

And therein lies its value and its charm: it's a terrific read in its own right, but it's also one that makes you think. Enjoy.

Introduction

Merry Baskin and Mark Earls

The scarcest commodity in the 21st century is attention.[1]

The idea for this book was prompted by our own difficulties in keeping up: with the latest ideas, the latest articles and the latest books – a sad fact of life for those of us whose professional success relies on our ability to know what is being thought by others, and building on it or going beyond it. Now more than ever the business world is deluged by information of all sorts, both on and offline. The world of business publishing has seen a renaissance in recent years, so that more books and magazines are now published than ever before.

We suffer just as much as anyone from information overload. Who has the time or the luxury to read (and keep reading) all that is written or uttered by our peers? Who can afford the time to read every issue of *Admap*? Of *Market Leader*? Of the *HBR* or *McKinsey Quarterly*? Who has the time to look more broadly into our culture and understand both what is happening and why? Who has the time to attend all of the best conferences and listen to and debate all of the best papers? And more selfishly, who has the time to 'feed their heads' with interesting new angles on problems, from neuropsychology, economics, evolutionary psychology or mathematics?

As heads of planning departments in large multinational ad agencies, we certainly found ourselves, as the Henley Centre would have it, Time

Poor (if not exactly Money Rich). As planners, people who are by nature curious and greedy for the new and the challenging, we were definitely finding it increasingly difficult and frustrating to keep up with the world. Moreover, we found too many of our employees and colleagues had given up doing so altogether. This worried us deeply, as the basic thinking equipment for account planners was developed at least a couple of decades ago.

Despite the information overload, we were conscious that some new and interesting lines of thinking were being developed that directly impacted on how we did our job, but too few people were properly engaging with them. Some of these thoughts were provocative, some of them groundbreaking, and a lot of them were just plain old-fashioned useful to us and our people in the jobs we do and the contribution we make to our clients' business success. All of them had the potential to make a significant addition to the basic thinking tools that our industry works from. To help our people do a better job.

Our ambition became this: to pull together these interesting new angles – with suggestions on further reading and what to do in practical terms in each area – into one volume. A compilation album if you like. *Now That's What I Call Good Branding Thinking* was one title we toyed with.

Some of these thinkers you may have come across before; some of their thinking has been exposed in different forms and in different places. But all of them deserve to be considered as part of the new consensus: that our concerns and obsessions of 10 years ago are no longer enough to get by on. That some of the old must be jettisoned or at least challenged if we are to continue to do what planners have been doing for the last 30 years or more for advertising and communications companies: make it easier for a great idea to happen.

This one goes up to eleven.[2]

Considering the long running success of the Account Planning Group's *Understanding Brands: By 10 people who do*[3] (now in its ninth reprint) we knew we could never hope to better the basic rule book of brand thinking. However, we could improve on it in two ways. First, by following the format of a collection of chapters but with an even more eclectic mixture of different thinkers (although one person manages to feature in both books). And second, by pushing the envelope of what the contributors chose to write about. The issues are bigger than just advertising and communications development. Indeed, one of the things that characterizes all of this thinking is that it starts from outside the brand world and works back in to challenge and reframe what we do and how we do it, rather than starting (as too many marketing thinkers do) from the inside and focusing on too much small detail rather than seeing the big picture.

Oh, yes – and third, by having eleven chapters rather than ten. Nigel Tuffnel, of the fictional heavy metal band Spinal Tap, would approve.

MUCH RESPECT

All of the contributors are people that we admire. All of them have at some point taught us to rethink our assumptions, and one or two have made our heads spin. We hope they do it for you, too.

As you read this book you will notice that not all of the contributors agree with each other. Indeed, there are a number of areas of dissent and contradiction in the following pages. This is intentional, for without it we would be creating a false consensus. A false version of the new thinking.

Nor will every chapter be to your taste: some you will want to put under your pillow and some you will want to tear up. Whether you agree or disagree with the content of a particular chapter is neither here nor there; the important thing is to read, think and feed your head with some fresh new thinking.

NOTES

1   Kevin Kelly, speech to IAA Congress, London, June 2000.
2   Rob Reiner, *Spinal Tap*.
3   Don Cowley (ed) (1989), *Understanding Brands: By 10 people who do*, Kogan Page.

Chapter 1

Learning to live without the brand (aka the seven-step programme to personal and professional liberation)

Mark Earls

Mark Earls has been called 'the London advertising scene's foremost contrarian'. He passionately believes that marketing and advertising thinking should move on from the old models and ideas – and he's not afraid to say so. A self-confessed platform junkie, in the last year he has spoken at the APG UK, APG US, IAA, MRS, AQR and Clio conferences.

He is also one of London's leading account planning thinkers: he has been Vice Chair of the Account Planning Group, judged APG and IPA Effectiveness Awards, been voted fourth in the Top 10 Planning Directors list by Campaign magazine. Somehow, he has also found time to write Welcome to the Creative Age: Bananas, Business and the Death of Marketing *(published by J Wiley and Sons, June 2002).*

Mark joined Ogilvy London in October 2001 as Executive Planning Director to help the London team reinvigorate its planning and strategic thinking, and is currently busy integrating all of the group's planners and strategists into one unit.

Previously, Mark was Planning Director at St Lukes and Head of Planning at Bates UK.

INTRODUCTION: ADMIT YOU HAVE A PROBLEM

The first step to recovery, they say, is to admit you have a problem (or rather a whole heap of problems). I'm happy to admit that I have a problem with the concept of 'brand': too often I don't understand what is meant by people who use the term and thus how to judge the soundness of much 'brand' thinking. Too often the 'brand' leads us to be backward looking. It makes us curators rather than inventors. It makes us lazy and smug and builds unnecessary barriers between us and our colleagues in business.

This chapter argues that all of these problems are a by-product of the success of the brand idea and how that success has come about. Because whatever else you want to say about the brand idea, it is nothing if not successful.

PROBABLY THE MOST POWERFUL IDEA IN THE WORLD

In his foreword to the predecessor to this book,[1] Don Cowley describes the brand concept as 'probably the most powerful idea in the commercial world'. Quite a claim.

Eleven years on, it seems that Cowley underestimated quite how ubiquitous the concept of 'brand' could become. 'Brand' has become part of everyday conversation among real people – they know that brands often demand higher prices and seek them out (hence the rise of the factory outlet retail concept in the United States and the UK, where branded goods can be bought at significant discounts). We are all familiar with the temporary signs promising 'designer brands at discount prices' – be it sportswear and equipment or everyday clothing. 'Brand' is the mainstay of the staged conversations between professional consumers and qualitative researchers. Both parties are more than happy to discuss the merits and demerits of brands, and play any number of games to mine for 'brand insights'.

'Brand' is also taken very seriously in the higher echelons of our culture. It has been the subject of a major, packed-out exhibition at London's Victoria and Albert Museum.[2] It is the subject of cross-discipline academic study in a number of fields; with the very public and successful 'rebranding' of the UK's Labour Party as 'New Labour', the brand concept has even become part of our political language, too.

THE VALUE OF BRANDS

Over the last 10 years, the City has taken a great deal of interest in 'brands' and branding: despite there being no real consensus about how to put a financial value on a brand, companies still pay over the odds for brands. The sale and resale of Orange in the global telecoms market is but one example of how much importance certain financial experts are now putting on brands and branding. Note that buying a brand is almost always done to enhance a company's ability to compete in different markets, not primarily or even partly for the skills of the workforce of the companies bearing the brand name acquired.

Some companies have long believed in the value of the brand. Coca-Cola is one of the best known: it owns the recipe and the intellectual property but not the factories in which its product is made and bottled. As one executive puts it, 'If Coca-Cola were to lose all of its production-related assets in a disaster, the company would [survive]. By contrast, if all consumers were to have a sudden lapse of memory and forget everything related to Coca-Cola, the company would go out of business.'[3]

In the fledgling e-economy, the whole notion of building a brand has proved useful: why else would so much of the money borrowed from venture capitalists be spent on communication but to establish 'our brand'?

THE BRAND AS AN ORGANIZING PRINCIPLE

Brands help pull businesses together. Many businesses in the early 21st century rely on a complex network of internal and external teams to deliver their products or service. In such companies, the brand has become a really useful tool for aligning the wide range of partners and suppliers inside and outside the company.

Hand-in-hand with this development, the discipline of brand identity has mushroomed, and with it the internal brand champions (or 'logo police') – those executives inside (and increasingly outside) the company who enforce consistency of expression and appearance. While the discipline of corporate identity is undoubtedly doing great things for many clients, questions are beginning to be asked – by customers, employees and the media – about the rash of 're-branding' exercises and their real value to consumers, employees and shareholders. The incoming Chairman (former Grocery marketing tyro, Allan Leighton) of what used to be the UK's Post Office Group – aka 'Consignia' – has let it be known that he, his staff and his customers would all rather still use the Royal Mail name. The £2 million re-branding exercise is now seen by many stakeholders as a largely negative and naïve exercise that avoids the real challenges in the business.

More and more examples are emerging of vacuous and meaningless outcomes to 're-branding' exercises that run the risk of making matters worse: Aviva (formerly Norwich Union and CGU), O_2 (formerly BTCellnet), Innogy (National Power) and Diageo (formed from the merger of Guinness and Grand Metropolitan) are all such alleged 'triumphs of style' over content.

A VERY MODERN IDEA

Whatever one's personal views about the doings of corporate identity companies, it is hard to deny that the brand is also a remarkably modern idea: it spreads and mutates as a concept with every victim/user so that there are now a myriad of versions of the 'brand' idea. You could describe the brand concept as one of the best examples of an idea-virus[4] in the last few years: like the open-software system LINUX, the brand idea has been given away free by its originators to all of us. We 'receivers' of the brand idea have been allowed (even encouraged) to add to and evolve the basic concept, which we gladly do with our brand essences, attitudes and personality tools. Each evolution gives each new user of the idea some benefit and he/she in turn passes it on to others to do the same again.

However, viruses are not entirely desirable: while the brand idea virus (or any of the variants which have evolved as the disease has spread) is useful (it helps so many different companies and individuals make sense of complex phenomena and challenges), the sheer variety of brand concepts has also become a hindrance to plain speaking and sensible business thinking.

WHY WE NEED TO LEARN TO LIVE WITHOUT THE BRAND

I'll be frank: I feel our 'brand-speak' has got out of hand. We're careless in the way we use the word (and as those with long memories will remember, 'Careless talk costs lives'[5]):

- We say 'brand' when we mean company, product, service, idea, strategic (as opposed to tactical) advertising.
- We sometimes use 'brand' to mean make or trademark, and sometimes to refer to the many and rich associations that our consumers develop around our brand names.
- Even when we talk of 'brand image' we sometimes mean that which we want to project and sometimes that which the consumer actually or historically perceives our 'image' or reputation to be.

The net effect of our laziness in using the brand idea makes most 'brand' conversations wasteful if not downright confusing. We appear to agree on the rules for the conversation, but underneath our terms are only loosely defined (and only sketchily evidenced). This allows brand-speak to be used by those who want to demonstrate a certain superiority over their peers; it is often a game of one-upmanship. When you use the word 'brand', you somehow seem smarter and more sophisticated than someone who uses the more prosaic alternatives.

But the real problem I have with the way people use the idea is that it gets us into dodgy thinking without realizing it: for instance, when we start to use the anthropomorphic extensions of brand-speak like brand 'personality' and brand 'loyalty'. I know what we're trying to say but I begin to feel on dangerous territory when we take these extensions too literally.

To be honest, I'm often confused by the brand-speak that we indulge in: my head spins. So part of the motivation for writing this chapter is to sort out some of this 'careless talk'.

BOOM-BANG-A-BANG?

Perhaps the confusion around the recent appointment of a high-flying advertising executive to help the US State Department 're-brand' itself is indicative of how silly all this brand-talk can seem and what murky worlds it can get us into. Under the headline 'Looking for love through branding', Secretary of State Colin Powell is quoted by *Advertising Age*[6] as saying, 'I am going to bring people into... the department who are going to change from just selling us in an old way to really branding foreign policy... branding the department, marketing the department, marketing American values to the world and not just putting out pamphlets.' Branding the State Department? Looking for love through branding? This way madness lies.

Equally bonkers is the recent attempt by HM Government to 're-brand' the British countryside. It was never branded before and is not branded now. Sure people have views about it. Sure, some of these are misplaced and unhelpful to the rural economy. And sure, we need to change public opinion. But that is not the same as 're-branding' the countryside. Bah!

THE BRAND UNDER PRESSURE

While brand-babble enters new realms of nonsense, the brand concept itself is under attack from a number of different quarters. There's the activist consumer movement – perhaps most eloquently expressed by the writings of Naomi Klein and the rioters at Seattle, London and Berlin – which is now focusing its arguments against the legitimacy of big business's practices on the brand.

> This book [*No Logo*] is hinged on a simple hypothesis: that as more people discover the brand-name secrets of the global logo web, their outrage will fuel the next big political movement, a vast wave of opposition squarely targeting transnational corporations, particularly those with very high name-brand recognition.[7]

Second, inside company boardrooms there is more and more scepticism about our brand-speak. Despite some high-profile company acquisitions being based on valuable brands, it has become increasingly clear that having well-respected and liked brands is not enough to guarantee business success; indeed, at best it is only just the beginning.

Moreover, our obsession with all things brand is driving us further and further from the concerns at the heart of the boardroom. This has been well documented by, among others, Tim Ambler of the London Business School.[8] In essence, he points out that as we worry about the measures of brand awareness, brand equity and brand meanings we are speaking in a different language from that which our paymasters speak. We brand-babblers are increasingly cut off from the concerns of commercial reality, and our brand-speak is further marginalizing what we do.

A graphic version of this point was related to me by a colleague recently: a young, highly talented (and rather naïve) market researcher walked out of her job when she discovered that brands – the focus of her work – were not just social and cultural phenomena, but of financial value to large corporations. While this tale can be dismissed as one of naïve idealism, it illustrates how easy it is to live in the world of brands and ignore the fact that, in addition to their cultural and social meanings, they are commercial items. Ask yourself: can you make the business case for your brand or do you just talk brand-speak? I believe we need to have a spring clean of the whole concept and our chatter.

THE BRAND IS A METAPHOR

Perhaps the most important step is to recognize and admit that the brand (however we define the concept) is not a thing but a metaphor. A way of explaining complex phenomena. A means of short-handing a whole host of issues. A linguistic tool. And like all metaphors it has its limits.

Two thousand five hundred years ago, Plato and Aristotle warned of the use of metaphor in rational argument because of their seductive qualities, despite their own repeated use of metaphor to explain complex ideas. More recently, a more enlightened view of metaphor has emerged: a number of writers have shown how important metaphor is to our ability to understand and express complex phenomena, both for our own benefit and also for sharing with others. In *Metaphors We Live By*, George Lakoff and Mark Johnson[9] propose that metaphors are not simply destined for flowery prose and figurative language.

> A metaphor is an invisible web of terms and associations that underlies
> the way we speak and think about a concept.

Indeed, metaphors shape the way we think and behave. The 'metaphors
we live by' are unique to our culture. For example, Lakoff and Johnson
demonstrate that we think of arguments in combative terms. So, we have
sayings like:

> She attacked every weak point in my argument.
> Your criticisms are right on target.
> If you use that strategy, you'll get wiped out.
> He shot down all of my arguments.

One of the most important tools of metaphor is the ability to objectify
and/or personify phenomena and associations so that they take on
concrete form and become things in themselves, separate from the
speaker. From the bogeyman of children's stories who 'embodies' a
child's fear of the night to the more complex metaphors used in politics
('this great *movement* of ours'), metaphors are psychologically, socially
and intellectually useful. This is surely some of what our brand concept
does for us.

THE LIMITS OF METAPHORS

All metaphors have limits. One is the accuracy of the similarity between
the two things compared. This is a matter of verification. However, the
biggest weakness lies in their claim to tangible reality. A metaphor very
quickly takes on a life of its own. It is out there, a thing, rather than an idea
that helps us explain the connection between things and otherwise
disconnected phenomena and our own feelings. We talk of 'the brand',
the 'brand image', the 'brand essence' and consumers' 'relationship with
our brand' as if it really was out there.

Consider Paul Feldwick's excellent description[10] of the 1989 Marketing
Society conference entitled 'The immortal brand':

> [The] publicity made prominent use of a quote from the Group Chief
> Executive of United Biscuits:

'Buildings age and become dilapidated.
Machines wear out.
People die.
But what live on are the brands.'

The visual design accompanying this theme was striking. The immortal brand was represented by a stylized, golden sun with a face on, perhaps reminiscent of an entertainment at the court of Le Roi Soleil. This rose above a classical montage of Greek temples, broken columns and Herculean statues. The metaphor [sic] is clear: the brand as deity, a sentient being whose existence transcends our merely human lifespan.

We do indeed behave as if the 'brand' were a tangible thing that existed separate from ourselves – a monstrous deity that demands complete obedience and regular feeding.

I want us to be clear when we use the word 'brand' – in fact, I'd like us to be clearer AND use the word 'brand' a lot less. To do so, we need to be clearer about the truths of brands and branding.

BRAND NEWSFLASH 1: THE BRAND DOESN'T WORK LIKE THEY SAY IT DOES

One of the least well evidenced but most commonly used assertions of brand thinking is the supposed connection between brand and behaviour: how brand perceptions relate to what consumers do in choosing between brands (or 'makes', as I'd prefer to say for clarity). In practical terms, this means: change the brand image and sales will come. As if by waving our magic branding wand over a so-so product, we can make it over as a shiny thing. And record sales and profits must surely follow. But things don't seem to work this way.

The first and most important fact here about how things actually work is that brand image and reputation (what customers think of us) change only slowly, particularly in response to advertising. Brand perceptions are built up over a long period of time. The latest advert or product is likely to have only a small effect on perceptions of the brand that have accumulated over 20 or more years. The one area that can change relatively quickly is the notion of 'currency': as Mike Hall of

Hall and Partners has outlined, 'a brand that seems to be doing a lot nowadays' – though I'd prefer we say 'a make that seems to be doing a lot nowadays'.

The second important fact is that brand image tends to change after behaviour, not before. Many brand fans point out the high propensity to purchase their brand among those who have the nicest things to say or the strongest 'bond' with it. Indicated action: make more people feel this way and their wallets will follow. However, the evidence seems[11] to suggest that – by and large – our opinions about the products and services we buy are a function of having bought them, not a precondition for buying them again. This seems to explain the strange phenomenon that purchase intention is a better indicator of the past than the future: of what I have done rather than what I will do.

That is not to say that the loose associations of thoughts, feelings and meanings that we attribute to different makes of things do not play a role in what we buy; indeed, without these associations and our knowledge that other consumers share what we think about the brand, it would be very difficult to use brands as shorthands to make quick decisions or for their social function. How can I make those millisecond choices between the 30,000 items in a supermarket without these kinds of shorthands in my head? How can I be confident that I am serving the right beer to my friends if I don't believe they agree with my perceptions of the product, its characteristics and its 'image'?

It would be just as easy (if a bit more long-winded) to talk about the 'reputation of this make of beer' or 'my past experience and associations I have made and I think other people make with this make of beer'. The brand metaphor just makes it easier (see, I told you it was useful...) to think or say this stuff[12].

The important thing to grasp here is that we use brand image and reputation to justify our behaviour to ourselves (and the army of market researchers stalking the land) and not as a precondition for future behaviour. Brand image is an expression of our previous good experiences and associations with that product or service, not necessarily an indicator of what we will do next.

In any case, most of the purchases we make are not at all important to us and are made at low levels of involvement[13] (much lower than brand managers would like to think, given the importance they attach to the purchase of their product). We largely buy the brand we did before because it doesn't matter that much and it makes stuff easy, NOT because we necessarily will die rather than use another.

BRAND NEWSFLASH 2: THE BRAND TIES US TO THE PAST

If much of the accepted wisdom about how brands work in consumer markets is false, one aspect of the brand metaphor that is particularly dangerous is how it ties us to the past. As we have seen, the brand image consumers tell us about (or rather the perceptions and associations they have built up) is a function of what they have experienced in the past (either directly or through third parties, like friends). In an important sense, the brand IS the past.

Much of the language of brand-speak seems determined to fix the brand-past for all time:[14] brand 'architecture' is surely designed to last. Brand 'essences' will clearly be around for ever. Brand 'values' and 'personality' clearly don't change. Except that things do change all the time. If the context changes around a 'brand' then its appeal will also change: how many 'great British brands' from your childhood have disappeared? I may still think fondly of Birds Custard Powder and its blue and yellow tin, but I don't use it any more. Mars' Spangles have been the subject of nostalgia in many New Lad publications, but a short reappearance showed that however fond we might be of a brand from the past, the product itself can still be irrelevant. How many 'designer' badge brands of the 1980s and 1990s now seem irrelevant and dated?

And brands change, too, but not perhaps in the way that we might think. As a result of heavy reinvestment in product design, Alfa Romeo is clawing its way back into the European automotive market, and as a result has a very different reputation from 10 years ago. By contrast, Citroën, once the design king of the European automotive industry with its Deux Chevaux, DS and space-age XM, is now, through repeatedly mediocre products, seen as tedious and bland. IBM is now a very different brand in important dimensions from its previous incarnation as Big Blue, largely through the acts of its saviour, Lou Gerstner (rather than its advertising alone). As a result of investment in new products, shop fittings and staff training, Clarks of Somerset are a very different shoe brand from that which Joshua Clark founded in the 19th century or the one that the parents of most of today's British citizens bought their first shoes from.

Of course, all of these now successful companies carry with them baggage from the past that is less useful – unsurprising given our long memories – but they have also changed their reputation and image over time.

So why is it that our thinking about brands clings on to the comforting notion of consistency over time? I believe that this is because much of the theory has been developed for and about FMCG brands. The central characteristic of FMCG businesses is that they are built on the premise of mass-production of a consistent quality product. Advertising and branding theory in this world are naturally imbued with the issue of consistency. You make the same thing day in and day out; you strive to ensure it has exactly the same guaranteed characteristics; surely, your brand should be the same?

In other businesses, the same hidebound ethos is not at all evident. In magazine publishing, the product is made afresh every issue. New content, new angles, new news. Every editor knows that however noble their predecessors, however glorious the past of the magazine, the product must be remade and rethought every issue. Once this month's issue is closed, the task is to reinvent the product again for next month. So it is not surprising that in this world, the role of brand thinking and its tools and processes is at best marginal.[15]

But the real issue I have with the unacknowledged past-ness of the brand metaphor is that it makes the brand a pretty poor guide to the future: the one thing we can be sure about is that the future will be different from the past.

We have been trained to 'discover' and 'unlock the essence' of our brands and use this insight to guide our future action. This is the purpose of all those brand tools, like brand 'onions', 'pyramids' and 'triangles'. They make us lazy: rather than looking to innovate, to create new customer satisfactions and their resultant 'brand meanings' through our actions, it is too easy to interrogate and sit on our fat brand-pasts and do nothing. Think of the decline of so many powerful brands in recent years: what characterizes so many of them is the self-satisfaction they exuded towards the end.

BRAND NEWSFLASH 3: THE HIDDEN DANGERS OF THE EXTENDED BRAND METAPHOR

If you feel a little dizzy at my critique of so many brand certainties, hold on to your hats for the truth about the more tenuous extensions of the brand metaphor, namely 'trust', 'loyalty' and 'relationships'.

First, *trust*. The study originally done by the Henley Centre for Forecasting (and subsequently widely copied) has been touted as evidence of the importance of brands to business. For example, we are shown to trust certain supermarket brands more than we trust the police or teachers or the armed forces. To the brand-maniac, this is compelling stuff (particularly if you work for one of these companies, but less so if you work for the police) and perhaps the crowning glory of the brand metaphor.

But are we really dealing with the same *kind of trust*? We trust supermarkets to be good supermarkets, rather than enforce law and order without prejudice, corruption or violation of our human rights. While it is interesting to ponder what a Tesco police officer might be like, this tells us more about our perceptions and associations of Tesco than about what kind of trust is dealt with here. Surely, we are comparing apples and pears. Tesco is a good supermarket at the moment; the police forces of the UK are not having such widely acknowledged success. Remember also (given the big brand effect discussed above), that this probably tells us more about how many people shop at Tesco and their experiences and how few have experiences with the police.

Loyalty is another strange anthropomorphic extrapolation of the brand metaphor mixed in with some behavioural wishful thinking. We would like to believe that our customers showed us loyalty (if they felt about us like they say they do, surely they would?), but most markets are – when considered over sufficient time periods – repertoire markets. Indeed, Andrew Ehrenberg[16] has shown that the most loyal customers (in terms of behaviour) in most markets are not the most desirable customers, as they tend to buy less from the category as a whole than less loyal customers. His argument – that the less loyal customers are where profit growth is to be found – is endorsed by Edwina Dunn of Dunn Humnby:[17] 'It is the massive middle tranche where the profits are.'

So not only is the idea of brand loyalty more than a little confused, it is also unsound. As a result it can lead us to unhelpful strategies in business.

BA, for example, have spent their time in the last few years targeting the 'most valuable customers' (business travellers) while ignoring those of us who sit at the back like cattle. The discount airlines like Ryanair and EasyJet have since built strong and profitable businesses from these 'least valuable customers' as BA's business has declined.

And finally, the notion of brand 'relationships' is worth reconsidering. There is some truth in the proposition that consumers have something like relationships with brands: we all use makes of products to enhance our private experience of consumption and as social badges, thanks to their established and widely-held reputations. However, most of us don't really have relationships with things, but only with people. We might describe our feelings and thoughts *in terms of a relationship*, but that's what the metaphor is for. Apart from anything else, few (if any) of the 30,000 lines in the average supermarket are in themselves important enough to us to engage us for more than a few seconds, let alone to have a 'relationship' with.

However attractive the notion is to brand-babblers and corporations, business can't actually have real relationships with consumers. Businesses don't have the ability to demonstrate the key characteristics of successful human relationships: mutuality, intimacy and sensitivity. Anyway I don't want to have a relationship with my bank; I want them to give me better service, higher interest on my current and savings accounts, lower charges, and to cut me some slack when times are tough. And yet my bank continues to act as if we did have a relationship: it tries to be my friend (so the adverts say); it tries to get my name right. And I bet they have a customer relationship manager. But I know (and they know) that they are just trying to sell me more stuff with every direct mail piece that comes through the door. They think that if I think I have a relationship with them I am less likely to take my money elsewhere.

I am not alone. A recent study suggested that only a third of respondents would volunteer that they had any kind of relationship good or bad – with a range of major brands listed to them in research.[18] And in another study, more than 70 per cent of UK consumers agreed that 'loyalty schemes' (a key relationship management approach) tend to benefit the company more than consumers. This is an expensive lesson to learn after the fact: despite $10 billion investment in customer relationship management technology in the USA in 1999, response rates to credit card mailings declined by 40 per cent the following year. One study across a number of markets and categories suggests that such technology investment is less than half as powerful as people policies in driving profit.

Here's the long and the short of it: 'relationships' may be found between companies in B2B markets, but not between companies and individuals. Period.

SOME CONCLUSIONS: WHAT TO DO NEXT

The brand metaphor has been and will continue to be a useful one, both for marketing professionals and consumers. As consumers, the brand helps consumers make hundreds of decisions very quickly and easily; it helps them explain to market researchers the wide range of associations that they have developed for a particular product, name or company (as a result of past behaviour): and it helps us in business understand the complex ways in which consumers add emotions and meaning to otherwise humdrum products, often indistinguishable from their competitors.

However, the brand metaphor equally brings some significant dangers to our thinking as business. The loose and vague way we use the metaphor can lead to lack of understanding of what we are talking about and enormous overstatement of the importance of what we do and how things actually seem to work. In particular, it leads into very dubious areas around relationships, loyalty and trust. It can – and does – keep us away from the commercial realities of the businesses we serve and those that pay for our brand activities. It ties our thinking to the past, makes us lazy and provides us with every encouragement not to invent the future for our employers and shareholders, our customers and ourselves. But most damning of all, in so far as the metaphor leads us into dubious areas, it consumes far too much of our time and resources when there are other more important things to do.

SO WHAT SHOULD WE DO WITH THE BRAND METAPHOR?

One option (a rather brave one, I admit) would be to dump it, with all its virtues, but few companies or their partners can do without it: the brand metaphor is after all 'the most successful commercial idea of recent years'. Of more practical use to readers of this book might be a more considered response: learning to live without it. If only for a while.

Try not saying the b-word for a week. Or a day. Or just a whole meeting. If you can't last even this long, here are some other pointers that I have found useful in getting the best (and avoiding the worst) out of the b-metaphor.

Wherever possible, do without the b-word

Name things by their proper name to distinguish between 'product', 'make', 'name', and so on. One stepping stone to this is a useful exercise called the 'Bnard-ing'[19]. This involves replacing the b-word with 'Bnard' whenever you feel the need. Think 'Castle Barnard'. Thus, you can talk about Bnard image or Bnard personality or whatever. It serves as a marker that you are not dealing with the b-thing that exists in reality, but that you are using a metaphor. It also removes some of the sacred quality[20] which b-speak tends to attract, which you may find refreshing.

Whose b-thing is it anyway?

Be careful to distinguish between reputation and associations that consumers have already made with your product, and the image that you would like to project (see 'brand-past' below) and the means by which you identify yourself (the logo and so on). In other words, distinguish between the two main variants of the brand metaphor: consumer-built and manu-facturer-built.

Understand the significance of what people tell you

As behaviour precedes changes in image and reputation,[21] recognize that much of what people tell you is an expression of what they have done in the past and even sometimes a justification of what they have done – dare I say it, sometimes even a fictional justification. Users are unlikely to tell you bad stuff; non-users may not even care, but will make something up to please you. Remember, just because you can access it using whatever fancy research tools are available, doesn't mean that it is important.

Use it wisely, my child

Think of the Bnard as your inheritance from previous managers of the Bnard. Consumers have built up a view about your product and your company, through a long period of experience of your and other products, together with what other people have said and – of course – what advertising has told them. But don't use it as a guide to what you should do next.

Your job as today's curator is to pass on to your successor something even stronger. The key here is action: what are you going to do that will make the Bnard even more valuable and respected? The biblical parable of the talents should be your guide here. Don't be so scared about losing your inheritance that you dig a hole and do nothing with it. Do something with it. Of course, there's a risk that you might lose it all, but that's the way of the world.

Focus on ideas, not Bnards

Underneath every strong Bnard should be an idea about how the world should be. Think purpose rather than positioning. Think what you are for rather than what you mean. This gives a business or a product team energy to move forward. It also gives the consumer, so weighed down by an oversupply of choices, a reason for spending any time at all thinking about you.

IKEA for example is based on the premise that everybody should have access to the aesthetic and spiritual benefits of modern interior design. This sets them apart from mere furniture companies and gives them a Bnard reputation that is differentiated but not easily copiable. One starting point is what you want to change about the world as it is or is perceived by your customers. Where are you and your product going to take your stand?

Focus on actions not words

There is no market for messages, so forget what you might say about your product or Bnard for the moment. Instead, think about what you could do to generate trial and retrial which emanates from your idea. What single act would make your idea really stand out? A good place to start is the supply chain. What change could you make that would most clearly signal your idea? One example is the UK frozen food retailer who bought up 40 per cent of the world's organic crop.

Don't think about advertising as a means to transmit messages about your Bnard or product. Think about it as a way of drawing attention to your idea. Use whatever you can to make it worth consumers' while watching your ads (and passing them on to a friend).

Measure the important stuff

As I've demonstrated, behaviour (and thus sales) are the important things, for both you and the boardroom. Measure this stuff and do so carefully to fully disentangle[22] the effects of what you do from the contribution of other (often bigger and more powerful) factors.[23] If you want to, measure the Bnard stuff, like image, awareness and preference, but only infrequently, as most of these things only move slowly and most are indicators of the past, not the future. And when you do measure Bnard-stuff, think of what you find as the reward you reap for doing good stuff and changing behaviour. Not as the aim of the game.

NOTES

1 Don Cowley (ed) (1989) *Understanding Brands: By 10 people who do*, Kogan Page.

2 Jane Pavitt (ed) (2000) *Brand New*, exhibition catalogue, V&A Publications.

3 Cited in Arvind Rangaswamy, Rayond R Burke and Terence A Olivia, Brand equity and the extendibility of brand names, *IJRM*, March 1993, pp 61–75.

4 'The notion that an idea can become contagious, in precisely the same way that a virus does, is common-sensical... because all of us have seen it happen: all of us have had a hit song lodged in our heads, or run out to buy a book, or become

infected with a particular idea without really knowing why.' Introduction to Seth Godin (ed) (2002) *Unleashing the Idea Virus*, Simon & Schuster.

5   British wartime propaganda poster.

6   *Advertising Age*, 9 April 2001.

7   Naomi Klein (2000) *No Logo*, Flamingo.

8   Tim Ambler (1998) Why is marketing not measuring up? *Marketing Magazine*, September.

9   George Lakoff and Mark Johnson (1980) *Metaphors We Live By*, University of Chicago Press.

10 Don Cowley (ed) (1989) *Understanding Brands: By 10 people who do*, Kogan Page.

11 See for example: Andrew S C Ehrenberg (1997) How do consumers come to buy a brand? *Admap*, March, pp 20–24.

12 This link with past behaviour might well also explain the 'big brand effect': on tracking studies big brands tend to get more mentions than small brands – more even than their relative size would suggest – because big brands have more users (and lapsed users) than smaller brands, and big brand users also use the brand slightly more frequently than users of smaller brands. This phenomenon makes it important for tracking study companies to re-calculate much of their data to show relative image profiles of brands in any market they track, rather than just the absolute data.

13 See Wendy Gordon, Chapter 7, for a more detailed review of the latest understanding of consumer psychology and the implications for marketing and advertising.

14 See Virginia Valentine (2002) *Repositioning Research: A new MR language model*, MRS Conference Paper 2002.

15 That said, the late arrival of marketing and brand babble to the world of entertainment has led to some silly things: one major broadcaster is supposed to have fired its major ratings daytime stars, Richard and Judy, on the basis of four group discussions.

16 For an overview of his outstanding contribution to our understanding of this and related issues see M Earls (2002) *Welcome to the Creative Age: banas, business and the Death of Marketing*, Wiley, and Andrew S C Ehrenberg (1998) *Repeat Buying*, Charles Griffin.

17 Quoted in Alan Mitchell (2002) Why the less valuable may be worth a lot more, *Marketing Week*, 7 March.

18 Source: Impiric self published.

19 Readers will note that this is an anagram of 'brand'.

20 See Feldwick in *Understanding Brands* (see note 10).

21 If in doubt here, revisit p 11 above where this counter-intuitive truth is explained.

22 In the UK, the IPA have championed the use of econometric modelling as a useful tool in doing this. See *AdWorks* vols 1–11 for some very good examples.

23 In my experience of analysing all kinds of marketing mixes in all kinds of markets, what the company does (in terms of marketing and advertising) normally ranks only fourth or fifth in terms of the most important factors influencing sales. Far more important are environmental factors like the economy, weather and competitors. If you don't believe this, think again: unless you have a majority share of marketing activity (say 75–80 per cent of adspend) then your competitors outgun you and their activity is likely to take sales from you unless they are growing the market.

Chapter 2

Giving up the ghost in the machine: how to let brands speak for themselves

Adam Stagliano and Damian O'Malley

*Adam Stagliano and Damian O'Malley are founding directors and principal
brand architects of Brand Architecture International, an end-to-end branding
consultancy within TBWA Worldwide with offices in New York, Dublin,
London and Paris. BAI was created in 2001 by the merger of Weiss Stagliano
Partners, New York, an advertising and branding agency, and O'Malley and
Hogan, Dublin, a brand architecture consultancy.*

Mr Stagliano was President/Chief Strategic Officer of Weiss Stagliano Partners, the first US agency with an account planner as founding partner and whose client roster was described as 'a who's who of premier international brands'. A founding board member and co-Chair of the APG US, he is also a founder and past Chair of the AAAA Account Planning Committee and a past board member of the Advertising Research Foundation. He holds a degree in Philosophy from Haverford College, and pursued graduate studies in Philosophy at Bryn Mawr.

Mr O'Malley was a founding director of O'Malley and Hogan, cited as 'among the first of a new breed of companies dealing with brand architecture'. He began his career in the planning department at Boase Massimi Pollitt, London, after graduating from Wadham College, Oxford. Named as Account Planner in Campaign's Fantasy Agency of the last 30 years, he is an honorary life member of the APG UK, and a founding board member and past Chair of the AAAA Account Planning Committee and the APG US. He has contributed numerous articles on branding and brand architecture to publications including Admap and the Advertising Encyclopedia.

Misunderstanding of the dream. In ages of crude primeval culture man believed that in dreams he got to know another world; here is the origin of all metaphysics. Without the dream one would have found no occasion for a division of the world. The separation of mind and soul, too, is related; also the assumption of a quasi-body of the soul which is the origin of all belief in spirits and probably also all belief in gods. The dead live on for they appear to the living in dreams: this inference went unchallenged for many thousands of years.
Nietzsche, Human, All-Too-Human (1872)

Buildings age and become dilapidated. Machines wear out. People die. But what live on are the brands.
Group Chief Executive, United Biscuits, Marketing Society Conference, The Immortal Brand (1989)

INTRODUCTION: BRANDS, A GHOST STORY

For many years now we've harboured a nagging suspicion that something was not quite right with the way we had come to talk about brands and think about branding. We began to notice a peculiar turn leading us inexorably down a path toward having us separate how we define the 'essence' of brand and how a brand actually behaved in the real world. We had become captives of a myth of our own creation – the myth of the disembodied brand.

Just how the myth came to take hold is not difficult to unravel. Following notions akin to David Acker's – 'A brand is much like a box in someone's head' – we searched for ever more clever ways and means of getting inside the head of the consumer and devised ever more elaborate boxes in which to place our brand. The metaphor of the brand-as-essence (and related, often anthropomorphic, concepts such as brand 'personality') derived from the 'voice of the consumer' became second nature (which goes a long way in explaining how the terminology in question became so entrenched).

Myths and metaphors persist not because they are true but because they help us to navigate the world in much the way fairy tales help to teach children about good and evil. They work not because they are any more real than say unicorns or dragons, but because in the ordinary language of everyday life they make sense and, in turn, help us to make sense of things. There are cases however when a myth or a metaphor becomes not a help but a hindrance, as when it assumes the posture and pose of dogma – schemes of conventional wisdom that we no longer require yet can't seem to shake the habit of. Sometimes this occurs without our even knowing it.

As we all know all too well, the world of brands has more than its fair share of myths, metaphors and dogmas. Some are quite useful, if benign. We would argue that the metaphor of an *Über*-essence residing above and beyond the brand as actually experienced has become the prime mover of a dominant myth of a more virulent kind – an anachronistic, if not dysfunctional, dogma that needs to be cast aside like a ladder we no longer need.

The key to this, we would argue, is conceiving of brands as actions, not artefacts; as enactments, not espousals; as behaviours not essences; in a word, as machines without ghosts.

MIND OVER MATTER (AND OTHER BRAND DOGMAS)

In *The Concept of Mind* (1949), Oxford philosopher Gilbert Ryle presented his classic 'ghost in the machine' critique of the dualist dogma of separating mind and body. Just how the mind, comprising immaterial mental states (the ghost), and the body it somehow inhabits, comprising material physical processes (the machine), relate to and interact with one another is the nub of some of the most intractable problems to bedevil modern philosophy.

Some have gone so far as to suggest that the mind–body problem – the problem of giving coherent account of the relationship, logical and otherwise, between categories of mind and matter – is among those 'world knots', conundrums beyond our capacity to resolve. Others have deployed all manner of so-called translation schemes – metaphysical, linguistic, even neuro-physiological – to describe the mind/body nexus.

The conceptual thorn that twists in the side of each, however, has been the failure to arrive at a satisfactory explanation of the causal relationship between the two sorts of entities, different in kind and residing in different domains. In cutting against the grain of the whole of the dualist tradition,

Ryle's 'ghost in the machine' argument is among the most derisive in its rhetoric, the most radical in its implications, and the most disarming in its simplicity.

The real problem as he saw it was in our misrepresenting the nature of the problem to begin with. The issue is not how we might give a reasonable account of the mind–body nexus but rather our tenacious but unreasonable assumption that there are two separate entities of similar stature in need of 'uniting'. In finding it hard to resist the metaphoric picture of a disembodied mind – a private black box in which all mental activity occurs – we have bewitched ourselves into believing that the metaphor is reality.

That we find it seductive to think and convenient to talk in terms of such 'inner ghostly events' says a good deal about our embedded linguistic biases and entrenched cultural conventions. It should not in any way confer upon them an independent reality detached from (let alone having primacy over) the material world of behaviour.

In reality there is no problem for Ryle, or rather, he re-framed it as a pseudo-problem, a category mistake: in seeking to reconcile mind and matter we mistake the shadow on the cave wall, cast by the ordinary language we use, for the thing-in-itself. To dispel the problems of our misguided dualism we would do better to put the ghosts hidden within our metaphoric language back in their rightful place and focus on the structure of actions. In other words, we ought to give up the ghost – and let the machine 'speak' for itself.

How we tend to think and talk about brands has become captive to an equally persistent and equally pernicious dualistic picture of what brands are and how brands work. It is the image of the disembodied brand, comprising immaterial and 'immortal' essences (the ghosts) separate and distinct from actual brand behaviour (the machine) as enacted by the organization and experienced by its customers. It is our contention that this sort of language has created its own 'inner ghostly events': the very ghosts that have come to bewitch marketing and bedevil brand owners in ways that might not even be apparent.

That said, our problem with essence-type words stems not from the fact that they are metaphors; language would be a rather empty affair without them. The real trouble begins when we stretch the metaphor a bridge too far from its initial use into places it has no right to be. The brand-as-essence is a perfect example.

Originally, the notion of a brand comprising an essence provided a welcomed, if expedient, conceptual scheme allowing us to talk about brands and approach branding as involving a good deal more than the simple sum of a product's literal, rational and functional parts. In this sense it was an instructive device of considerable therapeutic value. The metaphor made sense, helping us to make sense of how brands worked. So compelling and seductive is the concept of brand essence, however, that it has graduated to the status among many marketing practitioners of being the one, true brand – the brand that really matters. The brand that like some mystical immortal soul is thought to 'live' above and beyond how the brand behaves (and the organization enacting those behaviours).

Similarly, the 'discovery' that people can be easily encouraged to think and to speak of brands in anthropomorphic terms, as in the proverbial planner's query, if Brand X were a person what kind of person would it be, has certainly provided utilitarian fodder for our getting inside (metaphorically speaking of course) the minds of consumers and their perceptions of brands. It is an unwarranted leap of faith to suggest, as some would have it, that a brand is, essentially, 'simply a collection of perceptions in the mind of the consumer'.

This human, all-too-human, tendency to allow our metaphoric devices to take on a life and reality all of their own comes with consequences often unanticipated, and perhaps unintended. Metaphor has its place as an analytic and rhetorical tool in the collective language-games we play when it comes to brands. Again, our objection is not to the game (which can be both entertaining and even enlightening) but to the fact that in our coming to concentrate so much attention on the metaphors we often seem to lose the point of the game itself, to the detriment of the very brands we say we care so much about.

Our solution is to give up the ghosts that have come to inhabit the world of brands, and let brand behaviour 'speak' for itself.

THE ESSENCE–BEHAVIOUR PROBLEM

The essence–behaviour problem involves far more than insider debates on the semantics of brand definition. In our experience, the 'essentialist' brand model has very pragmatic implications that cut to the very core of how we have come to frame brand problems, conceive of marketing best practice and devise business solutions.

Among the most significant (because most insidious) consequences of giving essence a misplaced reality is its tendency to focus marketing activities in an almost entirely self-referential way on how best to define and then to espouse the essence of brands. Espoused brands are the brands that live in brand plans, marketing documents and creative briefs populated by the likes of brand prisms and personality pyramids, and which find their expression in creative artefacts such as advertising campaigns.

The paradox here is that while the marketing department might 'sell' espoused brands, customers 'buy' and use enacted brands, just as they experience brand behaviour not brand plans. In a worst-case scenario, this may create or exacerbate dissonance between the brand espoused by marketing and the brand enacted every day by the organization – between brand pronouncement and brand performance. A notable (and all too common) case is when an otherwise convention-bound brand presents itself to its customers in convention-breaking advertising – as when, for example, a bank or an airline radically 'disrupts' its advertising while its customer interface ('humanware' as well as software) and its tangible product and service offering continue to behave in the same tired old ways.

Such advertising might well be successful in espousing a new essence (no doubt including some cognate of 'innovation') and a new personality (more likely than not 'friendly') but does it really contribute to a better behaving, and in turn, more valuable, brand? The issue here is not that the emperor has no clothes; rather it is the fact that the clothes he is wearing are entirely inappropriate to his behaviour – and the crowd knows it.

Another problem related to the essentialist model has been the tendency to derive the essence of the brand from the minds of consumers. Using consumers to drive brand definition – envisioning the brand from the outside looking in, as it were – has long been a tenet of the orthodoxy of marketing best practice. The perfectly good advice to 'know thy customer' takes a rather odd and dangerous turn when it morphs to 'be thy consumer'. The use (and abuse!) of account planning by agencies and clients alike has given further impetus to ensuring that the 'voice of the consumer' is followed at every step along the branding way.

For planners and all those with a vested interest in doing right by brands (and their stakeholders), customer focused behaviour is a necessity, and attentive listening to the customer, an imperative; blind faith in what he or she has to say is a different matter. It is as though we've become like Pavlov's dog, perking our ears up at each word uttered in focus groups and every blip on our research screens, until we can hardly hear ourselves think.

It is just this sort of misguided consumer-centricity that begs the question as to how far a brand should go to make itself in the image of the consumer: at what point does a brand become simply a mirror (and often a rear-view one at that!) of the consumer's self-image? In other words, have brands become so fixated on reflecting the consumer's sense of self that they have lost sight of their own?

One has only to look at the generic visual and verbal vocabulary with which brands so often present themselves today to detect the effects of staring too long in the consumer's mirror. With everyone asking the same sorts of questions of the same sorts of people, applying the same sorts of research methods and metrics, is it any wonder that brand essences, let alone communications (if not products themselves) risk blending and blurring into a banal tide of 'relevance' and homogeneity? It would be an ironic twist of fate if branding, originally devised to de-commoditize products, to literally 'brand' a product with a distinctive mark, would unwittingly return brands to commodity status.

The all-too-excessive cult of the consumer only serves to perpetuate a *modus operandi* that would have us following rather than leading customers and, in turn, failing to capture their attention, let alone inspire their imagination. In the hyperdrive world of media and messages our customers inhabit, safe and sound is usually neither.

One of the things that make the essence model so appealing is no doubt its apparent simplicity. An essence is a distillation, a literal reduction to the heart (or soul) of the matter. On the surface of things, this seems like a perfectly reasonable way of helping us to make sense of the 'bloomin', buzzin' confusion' surrounding brands. The fact is, however, that brands are complex, and branding is a complex process. Indeed, it was with the aid of conceptual tools like brand essence that we came to see that even a soap powder is no more just the powder in the box than Guinness is just the beer in the glass, or Rolex just the dial on the face of a watch. But in replacing the old and limiting product-centric perspective with an essence-centric one, we have changed the bathwater and thrown out the baby.

In the real world, brands act as a complex and steady-state stream of verbs, not the simplified nouns and adjectives espoused in brand essence exercises. In other words, a brand is as a brand does, and what it does is an experience of irreducible complexity – multidimensional, multilayered, and often polysensual. And as with a *grande complication* watch that tells us quite a bit more than the time of day, the pleasure and value a brand delivers is often derived from the complexity itself. Satisfying the emotions, reason, aesthetics, memory, all at once, is not a simple task and does not admit of simple solutions.

Of course there is nothing inherently wrong in our urge to simplify, particularly when the motive is greater clarity of thought and precision of action. But when we reduce complexity for the sake of expedience, it can become an exercise in bad faith – choosing to see what is not there or choosing to not see what is there. Defining brands as distillates of generic essences and personalities might simplify advertising briefs but has little to do with the enacted world of brands. Somehow one doubts that Frank Gehry worked to a brief of 'sturdy, stylish, and big', when envisioning the Guggenheim (a remarkably well-enacted brand in itself) in Bilbao.

Similarly, when Jean-Marie Dru suggested in *Disruption* (1996) that 'we must refuse to accept simplification and the banalization that ensues', he challenged us to challenge the conventional marketing wisdom that equates simpler with better, simplest with best. 'For advertising people accustomed to simplifying, that's a rather disruptive thought.' Disruptive indeed, particularly to those who put their faith in the simplicity of ghosts in the machine.

A further, and to our way of thinking, the most egregious, consequence of the essentialist model is the fact that generally speaking, marketing departments, the *de facto* keepers of the brand, all too often live within the virtual Chinese Walls that stand between the black box of their disembodied brands and all other organizational disciplines, functions and activities effectively concerned with enacted brand management.

Yet if brands are indeed a consequence of organizational behaviours, then 'you are what you do, not what you say'; or better yet, what you say – that is, communications – ought to be thought of as a particular kind of behaviour – a speech-act, so to speak. Good and great brands do not simply espouse their way to market on the wings of their ghostly essences, led by the nose of their consumers. Rather, as Scott Bedbury of Nike and Starbucks fame would have it, 'they *act* as the great protagonists of our time... raising the bar on *the experience* for an entire category' (italics ours).

Brands are what they are (and can be) because of all the ways in which they behave, both operationally and in relation to their customers. Moreover, they do so as the result of a consistent and coherent organizational will to act in particular ways that finds expression in every dimension of the enacted brand experience.

'Think Different' works so well for Apple because Apple behaves different(ly), just as Saturn was 'a different kind of car' because it was 'a different kind of company'. Operationally, functions such as quality control, product development and design, customer service, distribution management are as intrinsic to their branding as marketing. While advertising can (and should) be transformative, as Apple has aptly demonstrated, it is always in the context of transformative through-the-line organizational behaviours.

Striking a somewhat similar note in the 1994 Harvard Business School's *Brand Management*, David Acker reported:

> The successful European companies we've studied share one critical characteristic – senior managers drive the brand... and as a result integrate brand building into their overall concept. In contrast many US companies delegate the development of the brand to someone who lacks the clout and incentives to think strategically. Or they pass the task to their agency. Relying upon their agency leads to two problems. First, in most cases it creates a distance between senior managers and their key asset, the brand, the driver of future growth opportunities. That distance can make coordination of efforts difficult, a situation that can result in consumer confusion, loss of synergy and ultimately performance that falls short of potential.

Understanding brands and branding as a consequence of organizational behaviour suggests that the architecture of a brand behaving well must be bred throughout the organizational bone, not as a creation of the consumer and captive of the marketing function, but as an organization's sense of self and collective behavior.

BRANDS BEHAVING WELL (AND BADLY)

If we accept the idea that brands are not disembodied 'essences' but rather the consequence of organizational behaviours, then it follows that, in most cases, a brand is inseparable from the organization that owns and manages the brand. In other words *the brand (and branding) is intrinsic to the organization and vice versa*. This runs counter to the current idea that brands are detachable (immortal!) assets that can effortlessly be bought and sold. Brands indeed represent assets, and indeed the whole purpose of branding is to create value, but it turns out that brands are rather unusual assets.

Let's start with an obvious example, McDonald's. If McDonald's sold franchises to any old people, allowed them to design and decorate the restaurants in any old style, sell any kind of food without regard for quality control, and so on, would it be the global iconic brand it is today? Would the golden arches have become the stuff of popular culture and subject matter for a whole academic sub-industry, if the company had not maintained its total behavioural control over every aspect of the McDonald's customer experience? The answer is, of course not.

The idea of McDonald's selling its 'brand asset' to another corporation is as absurd as the idea of Graham Norton selling his name to Jeremy Paxman. (Even more absurd is the notion that McDonald's could franchise its disembodied 'brand essence' or sell it to an acquiring company willing and able to 'enact' it!) When it is put like this, it is obvious that it is hard to buy and sell service brands without selling the whole organization. What may be less obvious is that it can also be hard to buy and sell product brands successfully. One recent case in point concerns the US beverage brand Snapple, extensively reviewed in the January 2002 issue of the *Harvard Business Review*.

The bones of the story are that in 1993 Quaker bought the Snapple brand from its founders for US$1.7 billion and then, after a disastrous four years, sold the brand to Triarc Beverages for US$300 million, a decline in brand value of US$350 million for every year it had had it. Then, in 2000, Triarc in turn sold the company to Cadbury for US$1.45 billion of which, *HBR* estimates, Snapple accounted for between $900 million and $1 billion! In just three years Triarc had more than tripled the value of the brand. How did they do it?

In the words of John Deighton (2000), the author of the *HBR* case study, 'Triarc's executives understood and embodied the quirky spirit of the Snapple brand in a way that Quaker's marketing team never did.' Quaker had effectively bet the company on the Snapple acquisition and, 'Acutely aware of the make-or-break nature of the acquisition, Quaker's executives formulated a marketing plan that sought to eliminate or minimize risk. As it happened, though, Quaker's very risk aversion turned out to be the greatest risk of all.' Triarc, on the other hand, were willing to take little risks, in the footloose and fancy-free spirit of the brand. They were happy to make mistakes but in the words of Nelson Peltz, Triarc Chairman, 'All we had to do was avoid fatal mistakes, to make sure that each time we took a risk, we would be able to come back if the gamble didn't pay out.'

The Triarc management behaved differently from the Quaker management. They tried things and if they did not work out they regrouped and moved on. They tried new product ideas out on the market and then listened to the distributors to figure out whether or not they were a success. They tried out low-cost, wacky marketing ideas, very much in the idiosyncratic original Snapple style, which sought to make Snapple customers part of the marketing rather than a target of it. Above all, they believed that they had a unique sense of the brand which obviated the need for elaborate consumer research and slick marketing plans: as Marketing Director Ken Gilbert observed, 'I don't think that there was anyone at Quaker who loved that brand, and it takes passion to get behind a brand and turn it around.'

It is perhaps telling that both the chairman and president of Quaker lost their jobs because of the Snapple debacle and, eventually, Quaker did lose its independence: it is now a unit of PepsiCo. In a further twist, when Cadbury acquired Triarc it was a condition of the deal that the management team responsible for the turnaround retained their positions in the new company. As Deighton concludes, 'There is a vital interplay between the challenge a brand faces and the culture of the corporation that owns it.' Cadbury ensured that there would be sympathy between the two by acquiring both the brand and the culture at the same time.

The only reasonable conclusion from the McDonald's thought experiment and the real world example of Snapple is that branding follows a logic that is the consequence of organizational behaviour; in other words, that far from the 'ghostly essences' that lurk within the hallways of marketing departments and their advertising agencies, brands are behaviour. On a moment's reflection this is a perfectly logical proposition. Customer beliefs about, and behaviour toward, a brand are built up through successive experiences of the brand in use. Every behaviour of the brand contributes, for good and evil, to that customer experience. Consistent positive behaviour on the part of the organization creates the expectation on the part of the customer that future experiences will also be positive.

This expectation of future experience (and the desire to avoid future regret) is what is meant by trust in the context of the brand – though it is critical to note that 'trust' is another one of those words that has a tendency to lead us down yet another seductive, slippery slope toward mistaking metaphor for reality. The beliefs consumers ascribe to brands may be easy for them to articulate in language that mimics the language of human relationships but they are not of the same kind, and seldom of the same intensity, as those we have towards people (and in the UK perhaps dogs).

As noted, such anthropomorphism is endemic to the marketing lexicon and often serves to both misrepresent and overstate the reality of the 'relationships' that people have with brands. The fact is that however much we may like to believe otherwise, people use brands. For that reason they are usually far more than willing to change their mind about a brand and as the Snapple cases demonstrates, are particularly sensitive to negative changes in organizational behaviour.

Another counter-intuitive implication of the conclusion that 'brands are behaviour' is that a brand cannot in any real sense be launched, it can only be achieved. A new product or service is at launch merely a potentiality, or, in the proverbial words of advertising creative briefs, a promise. To put it another way, it is espousal not enactment.

If we may offer a final quote from the *HBR* Snapple case study, 'Marketers offer brand ideas to the market, but those ideas don't truly become brands until they are accepted, adopted and made over afresh as part of the lives of those who use them.' Just as the proof of the pudding is in the eating, a brand can only be created through successive organizational behaviours that result in a coherent and consistent customer experience.

Of course there are numerous holding companies that buy and sell brands in a constant game of diversification (as often as not followed by a further period of consolidation, as in the case of Diageo). Many would argue that belonging to a global family or portfolio brings multiple concrete advantages: such as global distribution muscle, access to investment capital, manufacturing expertise, and so on. Fundamentally, however, these are aspects of organizational behaviour and in fact underpin the assertion that there is interplay between organizational behaviour and brand success. This interplay is simply harder to detect in holding companies than in single-brand companies.

THE HEAD–BODY PROBLEM

John Lennon once famously observed that 'life is what happens when you're making other plans'. What he meant was that the making of plans is often incidental to the way in which things actually turn out. In the marketing arena we have fallen into the delusion that the plans and pronouncements that we make for our brands are what drive the creation of brand value. As we have already argued, it is the totality of people's experiences of the organization that actually dictates what they will think and feel about a brand.

Far from actually controlling the total brand experience, marketing departments are not built to embrace total brand experience as part of their remit; at best, integrated marketing is seen as a way to connect the various dots of communication activities. Conversely, while paying lip service to the concept that the brand is one of the company's most important economic assets, most companies do not organize themselves to manage their brands in a coherent way.

One of the factors that contributes to this is that companies lack the appropriate intellectual frameworks to relate the concept of brand to organizational behaviour. The brand is some kind of mysterious disembodied essence, described in picturesque images defined in studiedly vague adjectives that can mean everything and nothing. The notion that companies are rational entities (again, a seductive but misleading anthropomorphic metaphor, a dangerous dogma of the highest order) making explicit plans based on rigorous analysis, which are then executed meticulously, is deeply embedded in Western business culture. The stock market rewards companies that fulfil quarterly expectations and punishes those that deliver the unexpected. And yet, as any experienced manager knows, the art of business is very often the management of risk and coping with the unexpected. 11 Septemher 2001 was just an extreme example of the shocks to which companies must adapt and adjust day in and day out.

Henry Mintzberg, a business professor at McGill University, has made it his life's work debunking the notion that strategic planning is a rational business strategy. As he queries in *The Rise and Fall of Strategic Planning* (1994), 'How can this be, that planning fails everywhere it's been tried? After all, the reasonable man plans ahead. Nothing seems more reasonable than planning. Suppose that the failures of planning are not peripheral or accidental but integral to its very nature?'

Among the fallacies upon which such planning is predicated is the Fallacy of Detachment. He notes that in business culture, strategists and planners are often removed from the organization. Most companies are organized into a head and a body, where the head does the thinking and the body does the acting. (There is a strikingly family resemblance here to our observation about the duality of ghosts and machines, and the problems emanating from it.) Mintzberg argues that you should not and cannot divorce thought from action; that management by walking about and informal networks is actually much more successful than sitting back trying to plan for a future which, as Lennon said, is going to happen whatever you plan:

> Effective strategists are not people who extract themselves from the daily detail but quite the opposite. They are the ones who immerse themselves in it while being able to extract the strategic messages from it. Perceiving the forest from the trees is not the right metaphor at all, because opportunities tend to be hidden under the leaves. A better one would be to detect a diamond in the rough... or to mix the metaphors, no one has ever found a diamond by flying over a forest. From the air a forest looks like a simple carpeted green, not the complex living system it really is.

THE GRAMMATICAL BRAND™

If we understand the brand as the totality of its organizational behaviours, then we can see that the brand is actually what determines how the organization behaves in confronting the unexpected. In searching for a conceptual framework that would account for how brands really work (that is, behave) to replace the conventional essence-centric model, and in particular to help organizations manage themselves through times of change, or inflection points, we have applied the notion of brand grammar (O'Malley, 1994).

Generally speaking, a grammar is the implicit set of rules determining the limits within which something will act or can be created. In the context of language, these rules, some learned and some, academics now argue, inherited, enable language speakers to discriminate between sense and nonsense, or, to put it back into the behavioural context, between good speech acts and bad speech acts. The concept of a grammar is extremely powerful and general. In the book *Grammatical Man*, Jeremy Campbell (1982) argues that grammars underpin everything from perception to life itself. To quote Campbell, 'Grammatical man inhabits a grammatical universe.'

The concept of rule-based behaviour seems at first glance to be unnecessarily prescriptive and proscriptive, and yet this need not be the case. The grammar of the English language allows for almost unlimited variety in expressive speech, while still delimiting correct speech from incorrect speech. The rules of chess are simple and can be written in a few terse pages, and yet there have never been two identical games. Without rules there is simply chaos and incoherence.

By the same token, at some level coherent organizational behaviour is rule based. Clearly, though some rules are imposed from the outside, as by legislation, most of these rules are implicit. By attempting to make the implicit rules of organizational behaviour explicit, we can begin to examine the gaps between envisioned brand behaviour and enacted brand behaviour and, more importantly, suggest ways in which the organization can change its behaviour and ultimately create more brand value.

Grammatical brands inhabit a grammatical universe, and a brand that behaves well can be said to be behaving grammatically. In codifying an organization's behaviour, a brand grammar helps individuals in the organization to discriminate between good, or value-creating, behaviours and bad, or value-diminishing, behaviours.

SUMMARY: LAYING THE GHOST TO REST

Brands live in the real world not as the detached, self-referential 'boxes' of strategic plans and marketing documents but as the organization's sense of itself and all the ways in which it behaves. The brand grammar is a way to codify and make explicit that which is often partial or implicit. In the most fully realized brands the organization's sense of itself and its behaviours will coincide with customers' experiences with the brand. When this is not the case a gap will arise between the brand envisioned by the organization, and the enacted brand actually experienced by the customer (and other stakeholders).

This gap between the envisioned and the enacted brand is common to many organizations, and is caused in part by the inadequacy of conventional brand models, which tend to restrict themselves to generic and often vague ghostly notions of brand essences, souls and personalities. The gap is exacerbated by the fact that often the brand is perceived to be the sacrosanct domain of one element of the organization, the marketing department, rather than the responsibility of the whole organization.

The implications for those of us concerned with brands and brand marketing are clear. We must learn to pay attention to the brand as we find it, not to the illusion of the brand as a 'box' that we or the customer create. We must stop believing in clever words and modish images as ends in themselves, and start believing in the power of organizational behaviour and the grammar that informs such behaviour.

If a brand is behaving well and creating value there will be little or no gap between the envisioned and enacted brand. Marketing will either impact the whole organization or, better, the organization will be indivisible from its marketing. The ghost will have finally been laid to rest.

REFERENCES

Acker, D (1994) Should you take your brand to where the action is? from *Brand Management*, Harvard Business School Press

Acker, D (1996) *Building Strong Brands*, Free Press

Campbell J (1982) *Grammatical Man: Information, entropy, language and life*, Touchstone

Deighton, J (2000) How Snapple got its juice back, *Harvard Business Review*, January 2002

Dru, J-M (1996) *Disruption*, Wiley

Mintzberg, H (1994) *The Rise and Fall of Strategic Planning*, Prentice Hall Europe

O'Malley, D (1994) The grammatical brand (unpublished article)

Ryle, G (1949) *The Concept of Mind*, University of Chicago Press

FURTHER READING

Cowley, D (ed) (1991) *Understanding Brands: By 10 people who do*, Kogan Page

Stagliano, A (2002) The luxury of disruption, from *Beyond Disruption*, ed Jean-Marie Dru, Wiley

Stagliano, A and O'Malley, D (1993) *Account Planning and the Future of the Full Service Agency*, AAAA Management Series: Account Planning for Senior Management

Chapter 3

The company brand: looking inside for the vision

Colin Mitchell

Colin Mitchell graduated from Birmingham University with a degree in English in 1990 and started his career as an account planner at BMP DDB. In 1996 he moved to New York where he worked for Angotti, Thomas, Hedge and Cliff Freeman & Partners. He is currently a Senior Partner and Group Planning Director at Ogilvy & Mather, where he has focused on integrated marketing on global businesses, particularly IBM and BP. He has won both an IPA Advertising Effectiveness award and several Effies and has been a judge for the Effies and the APG Account Planning Awards. His articles on advertising have been published in the advertising press and the Harvard Business Review.

INTRODUCTION

Perhaps because the fashions and tactics that marketers use change so quickly, we are left with the impression that branding strategies change every year. Yet, if we stand back and look at the history of modern branding ('modern' being defined, roughly, as the period since the mid-1950s[1]), we can see that it has basically gone through three stages. Each of these is defined by a dominant focal point: the product, the consumer and the competition. Each stage was born of the marketing environment of its time, but each has matured into a school that has complemented, rather than replaced, its predecessors. There is some evidence to suggest that a fourth stage is now emerging, which in time will become its own school. This stage takes the company itself as its focal point. Of course, marketers and agencies will always argue that their brands are forged through the intersection of all of these strategies, but in reality each brand tends to have its centre of gravity in only one.

Here we look at the evolution of branding strategies, argue why a new one appears to be emerging, then offer some ideas on how to work with it.

THE PRODUCT STRATEGY

In the period before the Second World War (in business history, sometimes called the production era), it was widely believed that a good product sold itself, and indeed a large proportion of the products were indeed new and unique. (Even Coca Cola had only been invented in 1886.) New manufacturing methods had stimulated an extraordinary wave of invention. In 1908 alone, the Hoover vacuum cleaner, the Ford Model T and the General Electric iron and toaster were all patented. The exciting and obvious benefits these products brought made the subject of the marketing obvious.

The post-war economic boom in the United States saw a proliferation of consumer goods that were not entirely new inventions, and the sudden increase in choice meant that marketers had to work hard to differentiate brands one from another. The age of product difference was born. Often these differences were arbitrary: Ivory was 'The soap that floats'; M&M's 'Melt in your mouth not in your hands'. But the need for differentiation also put pressure on manufacturers to innovate. The extent to which advertising agencies collaborated with clients on this is sometimes now forgotten. J Walter Thompson kept kitchens to conduct taste tests on new products. BBDO kept 'technical departments' for product testing. Mobil Oil is reputed to have put detergent in its gasoline after listening to advice from its agency, Ted Bates. Research companies also collaborated. The Nielsen company advised manufacturers that if their product did not get at least a 60:40 blind test preference over incumbents, they shouldn't attempt to introduce it.

The high apostle of product difference was Rosser Reeves of the Ted Bates agency. It was he who coined the term 'unique selling proposition'. A perfect example of a Reeves ad (for Anacin) showed three boxes inside the skull of a headache sufferer containing a pounding hammer, a coiled spring and an electric shock which were soothed away by the Anacin bubbles rising from the stomach. Reeves made much of the idea of 'reason' in advertising, which sought to persuade consumers rationally of the product's superiority. The role of creativity was downplayed: 'Once you've found a Unique Selling Proposition, any good copywriter can write a good ad. The rest is just wordsmithing.' He later proudly announced that the Anacin ads were 'the most hated commercials in the history of advertising'.

Creatively, Reeves' polar opposite was Bill Bernbach, founder of the 'Creative Revolution'. At one extreme, Reeves aspired to make advertising a science: 'Advertising began as an art and too many advertising men want it to remain that way – a never-never land where they can say: "This is right because we feel it is right."' At the other extreme, Bernbach advocated pure intuition: 'Advertising is fundamentally persuasion and persuasion happens to be not a science, but an art.' Yet, despite this fundamental difference, the two agreed completely that the subject of advertising should start and end with the product. Indeed it probably never occurred to them that it could do anything else.

Bernbach's advice for preparing to write an ad could have come from Reeves, Ogilvy or any of the other greats of the time: 'You've got to live with your product. You've got to get steeped in it. You've got to get saturated with it. You must get to the heart of it. Indeed if you have not crystallized into a single purpose, a single theme, what you want to tell the reader, you cannot be creative.' And indeed all the great Bernbach ads (and most in the Bernbach tradition) have a very particular technique: they start with a product detail and dramatize it in a big, arresting way.

Volkswagen's 'Think Small' or the Avis 'Number Two' ads, for example, make a virtue of an ostensible shortcoming.

The product strategy is still very much alive and well. Proctor & Gamble still pursues it with great success and in the United States, most brand strategies can be said to fall into some variation of this category.

THE CONSUMER STRATEGY

In 1960 Theodore Levitt published an article, 'Marketing myopia', that changed business forever. The basic tenet was that businesses needed to be focused on the customer, not the business. Although this has become so accepted now that it looks like common sense, at the time it seemed radical indeed. Most companies were 'production oriented' (focused on how they could sell what they made) rather than consumer oriented (focused on what consumers wanted). The full impact of this idea was not to be felt for at least a decade, but the changes started immediately. The most important was the rise of the marketing department in both size and prestige, and the eventual presence of marketing people at the senior levels of management. One of the main tools that these newly empowered marketing departments used was market research, particularly in the development of advertising.

Ever since Ray Rubicam had hired George Gallup from Northwestern University to start a research department in 1932, agencies had polled customers' views. Yet the main purpose of this was to evaluate advertising, through various forms of pre and post testing. Starting in the late 1950s, it began to be used in the up-front process to inform what would now be called the advertising strategy. First attempts were crude. Borrowing techniques from psychology, the 'depth boys', as they were known, came up with insights that were either obvious or eccentric. For example, the most famous of the 'motivational researchers', Ernest Dichter, famously advised Chrysler that men thought of their sports cars as mistresses and of the sedans as wives. Initially a niche item in agencies, 'qualitative' research over the course of the next decade became mainstream as its techniques became more revealing and useful.

The most important discovery that the researchers made was that consumers' motives for purchasing were a lot less rational and a lot more emotional than had been previously thought. Many of the reasons that they gave turned out to be post-rationalizations for decisions that were made on whim or to satisfy emotional urges. These discoveries resulted in a shift in marketing emphasis, from what the product did to how the brand made you feel.

Soon these strategic changes began to be seen in the advertising, though one wonders if it was clear to the practitioners of the time what was going on. One of the most famous early consumer-based ads was Coca-Cola's 'Hilltop' commercial of 1971. The story of its creation is revealing. Bill Backer, of McCann Erickson, was delayed for a flight and saw his fellow passengers gather together drinking Cokes. His epiphany was that Coca-Cola was about the human relationships, not really about the product at all.

While this was going on, the great packaged goods categories of the 1950s, such as food, toiletries and cleaners, were maturing. Manufacturing processes had improved to the point where product features could be copied rapidly. Concrete product differences thus became eroded, and companies looked more and more to marketing to take their place. There was a general realization that while the product could be imitated the brand could not, so building an emotional bond with the consumer was the key to long-term profitability.

In the UK these developments were taken very much to heart. Two agencies in particular embraced the possibilities that market research offered. Stanley Pollitt at BMP and Steven King at JWT created a minor revolution by taking the agency researcher from the proverbial back room and making that person part of the account team (an 'account planner'), in order to feed consumer insights directly into the creative process. The effect has been long lasting. To this day, one of the main differences between American and British advertising is that a far greater proportion of British ads have been based on how the product fits into the consumer's life. Many of the great campaigns of the 1970s and 1980s grew out of this approach, such as Oxo, where the brand effectively is part of the family, or John Smiths beer, where it became a companion. Starting with Chiat Day in the mid-1980s, planning was embraced by younger, progressive agencies in the United States keen to differentiate themselves from Madison Avenue.

THE DISRUPTION STRATEGY

In the late 1980s a third school of strategy emerged roughly simultaneously in different cities around the world. Just as the consumer phase had been a reaction to the limitations of the product phase, this new stage was, in part, a reaction against what Jean-Marie Dru of BDDP called the 'excessive cult of the consumer' (Dru, 1996).

Several developments conspired to cause this change. The first was a feeling that the media had become saturated with advertising messages. Over the 1980s media had become very fragmented (in the United States the four television networks of the 1950s had been supplemented by hundreds of cable channels). Marketing messages had become ubiquitous, as advertisers had become more ingenious in placing them. Gargantuan statistics describing the number of messages consumers were exposed to daily were quoted. Brands had also become fragmented. Even Coca-Cola, that model of brand focus, had developed several different variants. Secondly, it was argued that, as a result of this, consumers had become more cynical and sophisticated. They routinely used marketing jargon in focus groups and were generally sceptical of advertisers' claims. They had also become adept at mentally 'screening out' these messages that threatened to overwhelm them. Technology had also evolved which made screening out messages easier, in the shape of the VCR and, more importantly, the remote control. Observational research showed that media was consumed often with very low levels of attention. (An amusing hidden camera technique showed the many activities people got up to when according to the audience rating services they were 'watching' television.)

Various agencies arrived at similar conclusions but offered different remedies. In London, HHCL argued that in order to have any chance of even being noticed, the advertising must challenge accepted consumer preconceptions. They deliberately set out to create advertising that disturbed or challenged consumers (in focus groups, rejection of a new concept was seen as being an encouraging sign; acceptance was proof that the advertising had not been pushed far enough). In Paris, BDDP coined the term 'disruption' and concentrated efforts on identifying the conventions of the category in order that they might be broken: 'Planning should be about encouraging difference. People usually value relevance; we encourage discrepancy.'

In New York, Kirshenbaum Bond & Partners talked about the 'epidemic of cynicism' that they observed in consumers and decided that 'persuasive marketing should be invisible'. They prescribed advertising that didn't look like advertising in order to get 'under the radar' of consumers. One suspects that the reason for this radicalism came in part from the need for these new agencies to differentiate themselves in the crowded mid-tier marketplace. Meanwhile, bigger agencies, while not embracing the philosophy across all of their business, used it selectively for image accounts.

Looking back, it seems likely that this phase was (perhaps unconsciously) influenced by Michael Porter's landmark work *Competitive Strategy* (1980). Porter argued that there were basically three ways for a product to succeed: it could be cheaper, focused on a niche or different. Translated into advertising terms, this put a huge premium on being different quite literally for the sake of being different. Creatively, this was a tremendously liberating idea and it energized the whole industry.

The new thinking also found roots in the idea of 'positioning'. Agencies had been talking about positioning for years. (Rosser Reeves complained in 1965 that he had never heard two definitions of the word that were the same.) However, it was perhaps best articulated by Reis and Trout in 1981. The basic idea was that brand building did not work in a vacuum, but had to take account of other (often more powerful or better established) brands that had previously planted messages in the consumer's mind. Positioning seemed like an answer to these new problems. By looking at what the other brands were doing and then doing something quite different, it was possible for a brand to be noticed and to carve out space for itself in the consumer's mind. 'Cutting through the clutter' became the marketing mantra of the 1990s.

One final, slightly more nebulous influence was the popularity of postmodernism, originally an architectural and artistic movement of the 1980s that by this time had found its way into the cultural mainstream. With its use of quotations and knowing self-reference, it further focused brand strategies on the media and competitive context of the day.

Two campaigns that typify this approach are the early Snapple advertising in the United States and the (roughly contemporaneous) campaign for Tango in the UK. Both campaigns reflected product truths (Snapple's natural ingredients and Tango's sugary, acidic 'smack'). Both also reflected the heavy user's attitudes (through the 'alternative' Snapple personality and adolescent style of the Tango campaign). However, what was truly original was the defiant way in which the advertising disrupted the conventions of the category. Sheer surprise was their most salient feature.

The zenith of this school arrived with the dot.com revolution of the late 1990s, when hundreds of new (often directly competitive) brands were launched overnight, and the need to establish brand awareness quickly overrode all other objectives. The decline of these brands (for reasons other than advertising) has done much to discredit this school of strategy, it seems, at least for the time being.

CONDITIONS FOR CHANGE

Once again things seem to be changing. As before, it will probably take some time for these changes to take full effect, but the early signs are here. Perhaps the most important force at work is the new roles that a brand is being asked to play. There are three that are particularly important.

The first of these is the brand's ability to strengthen stock price. A study commissioned by the American Association of Advertising Agencies in 1997 suggested that although advertising only had a direct impact on 5 per cent of stock value, it had an indirect effect on 75 per cent of the factors affecting stock price. This makes sense. Having a strong brand makes it easier for brokers and analysts to give a 'buy' recommendation. It also makes the stock attractive to individual investors, and it is easier for fund managers to explain why they have chosen a certain stock. The Cisco 'Are you Ready?' campaign is a good example of a campaign targeted both at potential customers and investors.

The second new role is recruitment and retention. In 1997 McKinsey & Company coined the term 'the war for talent' which found huge reso- nance with companies worldwide. In the information age a knowledge worker is one of a company's most valuable assets. Yet McKinsey's research shows that only 20 per cent of companies think that they have enough talented leaders to pursue business opportunities. A strong brand is a partial answer to this problem, because people want to work for a company that is famous and respected.

The third role is to give a rallying point to 'stakeholders'. (It is significant that we now often use this term in preference to 'consumers'.) This group could include distributors, franchisees, and business partners: the parties who constitute the company's 'value net'. In practical terms, this means that having a famous and respected brand makes it easier to do deals – to increase your distribution, form alliances and so on.

What all three of these new roles have in common is that they have little to do with the company's product. When appealing to these new audiences, the company has to sell itself.

Meanwhile, consumers' relationships with the companies that they buy from are also changing. Increasingly, they are buying the company rather than the product. This is due partly to the greater importance of service. Even General Motors, that archetypal manufacturing company, now makes two-thirds of its profits from servicing and leasing cars – it has, in effect, become a service brand. Financial institutions are encouraging people not just to buy individual products, but to participate in a long-term relationship in which their changing needs can be met by the same company over time.

The final influence that is encouraging companies to look inward for branding ideas is the greater consideration given to corporate culture recently. Culture is important because it provides both direction and motivation to a company. *Built to Last* (1994), a study of the success of 'visionary companies' by Jim Collins and Jerry Porras, was particularly influential because of its huge popular appeal and the way in which it convincingly linked culture to superior long-term stock performance.

A NEW STAGE: THE COMPANY STRATEGY

These conditions appear to be giving rise to a new form of brand strategy, one where the main focus is the company itself. Corporate soul becomes the inspiration. Although in some ways this seems like a break with the past, seen with the benefit of a historical context it looks like a more logical progression from the stages that preceded it. Table 3.1 helps illustrate this. Two categories for which this strategy is becoming very typical (and which can be said to be leading the way) are apparel and technology. Nike, The Gap, Apple and IBM are all good examples. This is not accidental. Neither of these two categories can use traditional branding strategies: their products change from season to season and so don't provide any continuous sense of brand identity; they have to lead consumers rather than follow them, and these categories move so fast that navigating using competitors' positionings is also impossible.

Table 3.1

Brand strategy	Origin/causes	Dominant idea	Focus	Typical advertising genres
Product	Rise of packaged goods brands/ early advertising philosophy	USP	Rational product benefit	Product demonstration; problem solution
Consumer	Erosion of product differences/rise of market research	Consumer insight	Emotional brand benefit	Slice of life; brand mascot
Disruption	Marketing saturation/ consumer sophistication	Consumer challenge	Competitive/ media context	Shock/surreal advertising; guerilla marketing
Company	New roles for the brand. Importance of service component	Corporate vision	Company's values and purpose	Anthem

These and other pioneering 'company brands' have some other characteristics in common. Unguided by other brands, they tend to lead rather than follow in their categories. They also tend to have rich cultures and folklores (for example the story of Bill Bowerman inventing the first Nike 'waffle sole' with the family's waffle iron). They have driven, charismatic leaders (often maverick figures such as Steve Jobs or Phil Knight) who lead with vision. Many have also had rebirth experiences, where bad circumstances have caused them to re-forge the company vision (for example, IBM's e-Business campaign or Nike's rediscovery of 'Just Do It' after the sweatshop scandal). In the future, not all brands that choose this route will have all of these characteristics, but those that lead the way seem to.

Location may be another interesting commonality here. A disproportionate number of brands using this strategy come from the West Coast of the United States, away from the traditional advertising bastions of New York or London. (This may be part of a wider cultural shift westwards across the course of the last century.)

The brand that can be said to have most fully realized this strategy (and so in large part invented it) is Saturn. Indeed the whole principle is summed up in its slogan 'A Different Kind of Car Company, a Different Kind of Car' (company first, product second). This piece of branding has been so influential that it has been mentioned in just about every marketing discussion since.

SOME TECHNIQUES FOR WORKING WITH A COMPANY STRATEGY

As we have seen, each of the previous types of brand strategy had its own dominant method of development. For the product strategy, the key method was study of the product itself, often through tests or factory visits. For the consumer strategy, market research was most important, particularly the focus group. And for the disruption strategy, analysis of competitive activity and positioning was usually the defining activity.

If a new strategy is emerging, it will develop techniques all of its own. For the truly great, truly focused brands these measures are probably less necessary. The vision of a Virgin or an Apple is so palpably infused into the product and the fabric of the company that much less soul-searching is required. (Indeed, less advertising is probably required.) For the majority, however, marketers and ad agencies will have to employ techniques to define and express the brand 'essence', just as they would with any of the other types of strategy.

The following are a number of practical techniques that have been found useful. For many years these activities have been done as part of a pitch process or as 'background' learning when agencies work with new brands. One of the big differences between this and the development of other types of strategies is that these activities will move from the background to the foreground. The good news for advertising agencies (and account planners in particular) is that many of the skills they have developed working on previous strategies can be brought to bear on this new subject.

Penetrate the corporate culture

This is fundamental. Indeed, if there is one important practical point here it is that the staff interview is the new focus group. These interviews should be conducted with people from different parts of the company: founders, managers, product developers, designers, service staff, all of them. It's also equally important to talk to recent recruits (on the basis that a new convert is the most zealous) as it is to talk to 'lifers' steeped in its culture.

Excavate the brand's 'archaeology'

One of the best ways to understand a brand's roots (which yet is done surprisingly rarely) is to watch the historic reel. Simply noting what the brand was saying when its communications were strongest can be revealing. Agencies in the UK have recently turned to semiotic analysis (a system of looking at the hidden symbolism of the brand) as an interesting lens through which to look at the historic reel. Andrex and Guinness have both discovered hidden brand properties in this way. Reading into the brand's history also helps. For example, Fanta, we learn, was born in the austerity of post-war Germany when the company had to use sugar beet (rather than cane) to sweeten it, and the name is based on 'Fantasie' or 'Fantasy'. These facts seem to explain much of the brand's *raison d'être*.

Another useful exercise is to draw up a timeline and plot the brand's advertising, sponsorships, packaging and other marketing history. This helps show the associations that these various activities will have left encrusted on the brand.

Several advertising campaigns have recently been built by resurrecting brand icons in a new context, including Lee Jeans' 'Buddy Lee' and Jack-in-the-Box's 'Jack the Clown' icons and Miller Brewing's 'Miller Time' property. 'Brand archaeology' can also inform product development. Recently a number of car brands have been recharged by bringing retro designs back to life, such as the new Volkswagen Beetle, Chrysler's PT Cruiser and Ford's Thunderbird.

Turn to the scriptures

Look at the writings of founders and leaders. Obviously, the larger the corporation the less likely it is that the agency will get time with the CEO, but there is usually a surprising amount that has been written by and about the company. If the company has written its credo, this should act as a starting point. Speechwriters are also a good source for understanding the corporate vision. The idea behind the IBM e-Business campaign was greatly influenced by a speech given by the (then) new CEO Louis Gerstner outlining his vision for the company.

Start with the brand, not the ad

It is striking how a discussion of the history of brands ends up being a discussion of their advertising. Until recently, for most marketers, brand and advertising strategies were synonymous. 'Below-the-line' activities, as they used to be called, were considered exclusively tactical. Then, in the mid-1990s, integrated marketing was developed (mainly in response to client demand for the efficiency of one-stop shopping). Ad people hurried to team up with their direct marketing (and later interactive) brethren. As it transpires, in the future integrated marketing will probably go well beyond making sure that mail shots and print ads look alike. Real integration will come through connecting consumer touchpoints as diverse as store design and call centre scripts, adding up to a 'total brand experience', as it is sometimes called. The Gap's casual, cheerful everyman style is as manifest in the store design and the Web site as it is in the ads. How different this is from, say, Levis, a consumer-based brand that lived or died by its advertising.

Work inside out

Internal branding is another subject entirely. But it is worth noting here that one of the main advantages of the company-based brand strategy is that it works as powerfully in galvanizing internal audiences as it does in persuading external audiences. For many companies the former is more important than the latter. Brands that work inside out in this way also have greater integrity. Home Depot provides a good example of how a brand is enhanced by staff who understand and believe in the company's mission. For it to achieve its potential, however, the company has to be as committed to both sides of the equation.

NOTE

1   The mid-1950s provide a convenient, if slightly arbitrary, watershed because several developments converged to make marketing after this point very different from that which went before. These included the arrival of television, an increase in advertising spending (fuelled by post-war American prosperity), the new dominance of the great packaged goods manufacturers, and the rise of the big 'Madison Avenue' advertising agencies.

  Prior to this period, discussion about marketing strategy had been dominated by tension between different creative styles in advertising. These basically oscillated between Claude Hopkins' 'reason why' or 'salesmanship in print' school (that is, advertising that is rational and persuasive, and usually long copy and direct response) and 'image' advertising (with its emphasis on visuals and 'atmosphere') pioneered by Theodore MacManus for General Motors and later developed by Ray Rubicam. In the post-war world, the Hopkins tradition was inherited by Rosser Reeves and the image tradition by Bill Bernbach.

REFERENCES

Collins, J and Porras, J (1994) *Built to Last*, Harper
Dru, J-M (1996) *Disruption*, Wiley
Levitt, T (1960) *Marketing Myopia*
Porter, M (1980) *Competitive Strategy*, Free Press
Reis, A and Trout, J (1981) *Positioning: The battle for your mind*, McGraw Hill

FURTHER READING

Bond, J and Kirshenbaum, R (1997) *Under the Radar*, Wiley
Fox, S (1984) *The Mirror Makers*, Morrow
Gregory, J R (1997) *The Impact of Advertising on Stock Performance*, American Association of Advertising Agencies
Levinson, R (1987) *Bill Bernbach's Book*, Villard Books
Levitt, T (1986) *The Marketing Imagination*, Free Press

Chapter 4

Brand communication beyond customers

Peter Dann

Peter's career in advertising started at Ted Bates in London, moving to Yellowhammer in 1986 and Bartle Bogle Hegarty in 1990, where he was Account Director on NatWest, IBM and Van den Berghs. In 1993 he moved into qualitative advertising research at Davies Riley-Smith Maclay, where he spent two years concentrating on developing the company's international research capabilities before becoming Managing Director in 1996.

Peter left DRSM in May 2000 to start his own company, The Way Forward, which, in partnership with Lucy Banister and Chris Forrest, became The Nursery in 2001.

Peter is a regular contributor to industry publications on research and planning in the UK and Europe, has spoken at conferences for the Market Research Society, the Account Planning Group and the Association for Qualitative Research in the UK and the United States, and tutors on group moderating courses for the APG and AQR. He was vice-chair of the APG from 2000–2002.

STAKEHOLDERS IN THE BRAND

In their prefaces to the hardback and paperback editions of *Understanding Brands*, Don Cowley and Alan Cooper both muse on the ubiquity of the modern brand. And no wonder: it is partly thanks to the wider public awareness of and interest in brands and branding that our industry has what stature it has and books such as this get written and bought. The rise of the literate consumer is well documented and now accepted as a fact of modern marketing: no-one cries 'foul' if they hear respondents in group discussions arguing about the merits of the brand strategy or panning the creative idea as last year's model. The disciplines of marketing, and advertising in particular, are now in the public domain where they belong, and commercial messages are rightly subjected to the sort of critical public scrutiny that stops huge corporations from having it all their own way.

However, while the trend is accepted, its implications on how we think about and manage brands are less well understood. This chapter will argue that, whereas in the past it has been fine to think of brands as sets of values and perceptions that exist in the hearts and minds of their consumers, increasingly they are 'owned' by, or at least affected by, a wide range of third parties. Indeed, not only do these people affect how the brand is perceived, but because it is often largely through their behaviour, values and opinions that the brand's customers formulate their percep- tions of the brand itself, they can play a more important role in formu- lating the brand's identity than controlled factors such as advertising. To use a millennial phrase, these are 'stakeholders' in the brand, and, like many other stakeholders, their stakeholding is not always beneficial, let alone well intentioned.

The implications for brand owners are wide. These days, when brands communicate with their customers, increasingly they have to take account of others: in some cases to enlist them in the communication process, in some cases to ensure that the communication is considered credible by those who deliver the brand; and increasingly, there are many brand communications that are primarily aimed at someone other than 'consumers' in the traditional sense.

Consequently, in addition to or instead of its customers, a brand may need to communicate with, for example, owners and recent customers, staff and potential recruits, shareholders both corporate and individual, resellers of the brand from dealers to shop assistants, even to its competitors or to society in general. Many of these audiences will have been addressed by someone in marketing for many years, but increasingly most brands should take account of most of these audiences most of the time. This chapter looks at examples of how this has affected some brands and sectors, and asks how the disciplines of planning need to evolve to take account of this new brand context.

THE NEW BRAND CONTEXT

Not so long ago, the UK and most other Western democracies were run by their governments. Governments formulated policies to direct the nation where they thought it should go, passed laws to effect the changes or create the conditions necessary, and unless something unforeseen like a war or a disgruntled electorate came along, they pretty much got their way. Today this is no longer the case, much to the chagrin of politicians. The ease with which capital, labour and pretty much anything else necessary for economic activity can cross national borders means that if big businesses don't like what a government does, they can go elsewhere and ditch that country's economy as they go. Politicians are left tweaking the edges of their economies, trying to make marginal improvements and shifting their societies ever so slightly towards ideological goals of the left or right. And to make matters worse, they now have to explain their every move to an increasingly empowered and critical media and electorate. Finally, if they're European, there's always the risk that someone from Brussels will make them change their minds, in public, usually at embarrassing moments like elections.

I would imagine any brand managers reading this will be feeling some sympathy by now. Indeed, the title 'brand manager' might evoke nostalgia for the days when a brand could be 'managed' by its owners; today, increasingly, brand management is also a case of tweaking around the edges, anticipating and exploiting contextual trends rather than autocratically directing a brand's progress. Increasingly, then, the context of the brand is as important as the input from the brand's owners; brands are as they do and seem, not just as they say.

The speed with which this trend has spread suggests that it is due to many factors. The media literacy that Cowley and Cooper referred to has

played an important part, but cannot be the only cause – after all, advertisers and advertising have become more sophisticated as well, often
keeping pace with their viewers. It is not just that people are more aware
of how marketing works, they are also more interested. Corporate news
that only a decade or two ago would have been consigned to the financial
pages is now mainstream material, and business strategies are analysed on
breakfast television. There are mainstream comedies set in marketing
departments and advertising agencies, and at parties qualitative
researchers no longer have to explain what they do for a living but defend
their methodology. Brands are more obviously artificial creations, and are
less likely to be taken at their face value.

The nature of brands themselves has also changed. From a world of
branded goods we have moved to a world of branded companies,
branded services, branded organizations – even governments. Life is
now branded: so it is no longer just my choice of car or of cigarettes that
projects my values and personality, it is my choice of bank, of mobile
phone, of vacuum cleaner, of frozen pizza, of supermarket, of television
set and television channel. And increasingly, these brands too are 'bought'
on the basis of a wider range of considerations. Price and product
performance are just part of the mix; we have become used to knowing
more about our brands. Where does this beef come from? Where are these
trainers made, and how old are the workers who made them? How does
this bank treat its rural customers? Is this new product made by a
successful company with a good track record in NPD? Who owns this
brand, and do we like the way they make chocolate? Is their advertising
agency any good? Is this name change of any benefit to me, or is it part of
a pan-European brand realignment? All of these are genuine questions
from genuine consumers reflecting a genuine interest in what lies behind
the brands we buy. Reviewing Naomi Klein's *No Logo* (2001), Billy Bragg
wrote, 'What corporations fear most are consumers who ask questions.
Naomi Klein offers us the arguments with which to take on the super-
brands.' But it wasn't brand terrorists who kept the book on the bestseller
lists for most of 2000 and 2001, it was ordinary consumers who bought it to
read alongside *Harry Potter* and John Grisham.

Not only have brands changed, so has our relationship with them. Most
of these new brands offer services rather than products, so we have a
different, more variable set of criteria to judge them by – their behaviour,
especially at point of delivery, becomes their product performance. Brand

behaviour becomes even more important because we have far more direct contact with these brands: retail brands are more affected by their stores and staff than by their advertising; service brands by the way they answer our enquiries; corporate brands by the way we interpret their actions.

Each of these trends is in itself significant, but together they have fundamentally changed the context in which today's brands operate. And this is the context that makes modern brand management such a difficult task, because, as brands have become more open to view, and subject to more detailed scrutiny, so perceptions of them are more likely to vary from individual to individual, with each consumer bringing his or her own understanding and interpretation of what the brand stands for. The days when the centre-break of *News at Ten* could determine the brand identity have gone, and with them the conveniently homogeneous research findings that can tell us exactly how the brand is seen. Consumers know more about the brands they buy, and see more aspects of them and the context they operate in; as an inevitable consequence, they see more disparities and notice the brand behaving differently at different times and in different places. However, at the same time, this greater knowledge drives higher expectations: consumers of most brands expect greater coherence in how brands behave, and demand even higher standards at all these different points of contact.

In today's commercial world, then, brand planning and brand management involve understanding and determining how brands communicate with and relate to all the aspects of their environment, not just their customers. But before we look at how these trends affect our jobs, here are some examples of the process in practice.

COMMUNICATING BEYOND CUSTOMERS

Past customers, distant customers

The market where the brand manager has perhaps the least control of his or her brand is the car market – and noticeably less as the value of the car in question increases. The reason why is simple: the car is most people's biggest single purchase after a house, and it is a purchase that is difficult to correct if you make the wrong choice. The result is that when contemplating buying a car, people with no interest in cars or engineering will spend days visiting showrooms, reading magazines, phoning friends, taking test drives and generally immersing themselves in the motoring world.

In a market like this, the most powerful brand communications can seem insignificant when pitted against motoring reviews, personal observations and – most importantly – advice from friends and colleagues. We don't have to go as far as the legendarily awful Ford Edsel to find instances of word of mouth or press reviews driving perceptions of a car brand: most Europeans' first knowledge of the Mercedes A-Class was that it fell over going round corners; a *Which?* survey reported that less than half of all Discovery owners would recommend their car to a friend.

Car marketers know this of course, which is why the target audience for much car advertising is not 'customers' in the sense of people about to buy a new car, but existing customers – owners – of the brand. More than in any other market, satisfied customers are essential for a successful car brand, because they will be asked their opinion and freely give it. But marketing can't create satisfied customers; that's the job of the designers and engineers. What it can do is remind owners of why they bought the car in the first place: those brand values are as relevant now as they always were, if not more so, given the need to justify your purchase to friends and colleagues.

This is particularly true when the brand in question does not have a particularly well established image for its customers to hang their hats on, in the absence of which their choice can seem at best brave, at worst contrary. Everyone knows what it means to be a BMW or Mercedes driver, but it took a campaign as single-minded as 'The Aircraft Company', a campaign primarily targeted at existing owners, to give the Saab brand a meaning that allowed owners to be openly proud of their cars. For Audi, the original 'Vorsprung durch Technik' campaign united a collection of solid but uninspiring engineering attributes into a brand that owners were suddenly able to articulate. The group most delighted with Volvo's shift towards more exciting imagery in the 1990s was Volvo owners themselves, who are currently telling their friends and family just how exciting their new model is to drive.

There are lessons for us all from the car market, as all brands become more like car brands in that their consumers increasingly know more and want to find out more about them. As with cars, what the brand can credibly claim is more and more limited by what it does and how it does it.

So also customers play an important part in brand perception – not just in their power of referral, but in what their choice (and who they are) says about the brand.

Staff – the brand brought to life

In a world where only goods were branded, customers could hardly be described as having a 'relationship' with the brand, although many brand owners liked to think otherwise. Brands lived on shelves in shops and supermarkets and in the home, and if you didn't like them you didn't have a conversation with them about their shortcomings, you just didn't buy them again. The one person you might have had a conversation with would be the shopkeeper you bought the brand from in the first place.

Today's brands are different. They are service brands, retail brands and brands that you can meet. And, hardly surprisingly, we put more faith in our own experience of the people we meet than in what advertising tells us. For example, for many years, banks struggled with the awful gap between the happy, smiling, building-society-esque imagery they could portray in advertising and the reality of poorly-trained tellers and ogre-like managers that represented the brand in real life. The smart retail brands (as most banks now are) realized that their staff were, at the point the customer met them, the real embodiment of the brand, and invested in training and recruitment as well as just marketing.

Supermarkets have changed the world of brands in many ways, but none more so than in how customers relate to, and have conversations with, brands. People still want to have some sort of a two-way dialogue with their shopkeepers: they want to be sure that they stock the goods they want at a fair price, they want advice on difficult choices, and they want to be able to complain if something isn't up to the standard it was sold as. But supermarkets are brands too, and in most cases every bit as powerful as any of the brands stocked on their shelves. The difference is that they can't hide behind fancy packaging and happy advertising: a retail brand is as its customers find it: its location and design of store, its car park and trolleys, its coffee shop and lavatories, its stock and its prices, and above all, its staff. No coincidence, then, that the big supermarket brands are in the forefront of 'transparent' brand marketing – they couldn't have it any other way.

Tesco's celebrated 'Dotty' campaign is a fine example. In the early days of the store's drive up-market, we saw Dudley Moore as the store buyer on his roving quest for free-range chickens – a campaign that challenged outdated perceptions about Tesco's lack of quality by talking purely about product quality. It was up to the viewer to look at their store afresh in the light of this reappraisal. But with Prunella Scales's Dotty character, the advertising shows a reality of the brand that is heightened only for comic effect. Most importantly, the campaign focuses on the point of interaction between the brand and its customers – the staff in the stores; and in the Dotty campaign we see these representatives of the brand meeting all of the most demanding customer's requirements. Tesco knows that it is down to members of staff to deliver the levels of service the brand promises. To quote Lowe's award-winning IPA (2000) effectiveness paper:

> Since 'Every Little Helps' was introduced in 1993 the advertising has been a very public statement of the kind of experience Tesco will deliver in-store. The strategy can only be successful in securing loyalty (and satisfying new customers) if consumers see it in action. Hence, it is essential that staff believe in the advertising and deliver accordingly.

Tesco's staff are not the primary target audience of the campaign, but it could be argued that they are more than that – they are part of it. Without the full endorsement of staff themselves, the campaign would be dead in the water (and, to the credit of Tesco's staff, few others would dare try it). On the one hand, it sets a standard for staff to live up to, but on the other, it is seen as a public recognition of the importance of their role.

What Tesco's campaign has done is to galvanize a whole organization into a brand. Customers know what to expect from the brand, and are delighted when the promise is delivered. Equally, staff know that they are the brand, and that their performance is critical to the brand's success. As the IPA paper quotes a Tesco employee with 26 years' service as saying, 'Twenty-six years ago I'd say I worked in a shop. Now I say I work for Tesco.'

Not all brands can afford to, or would want to, communicate so openly with their staff or involve them so publicly in their external communications, but what we can learn from Tesco and from other staff-focused organizations is how powerful that interaction between staff and customers can be. The effect of expectations of interaction go further than retail and service brands – people expect to be able to have a dialogue with more and more brands, and expect the brand to be consistent however they make contact with it. The 'shopkeeper' as the point of dialogue has been replaced not just by the supermarket staff but by the call centre workers, the engineers, the van drivers, the Web site and the factories themselves. Brand communications that at least acknowledge these living parts of the brand have a head start on those that try to skip over the points of delivery and talk to customers purely on their own terms.

Reaching out beyond the brand – recruiting

If the brand's employees are seen as the most accurate expression of the brand itself, then the sort of employees the brand is seen to want to attract gives a clear indication of what the brand wants to be. Much like any brand communication, then – except that in this case, there is a real sense of commitment to that vision. If the brand really is going to recruit (and retain) these sorts of people, then the vision can't just be a creation of the marketing department; it must have some degree of follow-through in the rest of the organization.

Organizations that have no customers as such shouldn't really have need of a brand, but in a competitive recruitment market that is exactly what most organizations do have, and the effect of their recruitment communication on perceptions of that brand is critical for them, and instructive for the rest of us. The armed forces, and the Army in particular, make good examples because – like many consumer brands – they are fighting against a momentum of public opinion that is not where the brand would like it to be.

In recruitment terms, the Army has long had the more difficult task of the armed forces: it is widely assumed that joining the Navy or the RAF leads to a life of high-tech weaponry and globe-trotting missions, whereas the poor Army squaddie spends his or her time yomping through muddy moorland with a huge back-pack and an earful from the Sergeant Major. No matter how exciting the shots of tanks and helicopters, there is always the camouflage to remind you that the mud is not far behind.

Since the mid-1990s, however, the focus of the Army's recruitment advertising has been not on the excitement of using modern weapons but on the level of skill and personal abilities a soldier in the modern Army needs; not on the glamour of serving abroad but on the difficulties and challenges these missions bring. Moreover, rather than attempting to sell itself to potential recruits, Army advertising deliberately takes the challenge to them – do you have what it takes? These have the effect of forcing people to reassess the Army's worth as an organization in the light of their own abilities, and to appreciate the role of a modern soldier as a skilled, quick-witted decision maker backed up by thorough training.

Of course, brand transparency applies as much to the Army as to any other of our examples: especially with such obvious tabloid fodder as equal opportunities stories and punishing training regimes. Indeed, the challenges and dangers that made some of the executions so appealing to many actively dissuaded others; but these will mostly have been those for whom a career in the Army would have been a disaster for both parties.

However, potential recruits are increasingly prepared to think of a job in the Army as a career rather than a last resort, and while a significant portion of the population will never consider it, at least they are less likely to laugh when their friends suggest it. Of course, brand transparency works both ways, and there are (and have to be) many real examples of how the Army has indeed become a more modern, career-focused organization, but, as with Tesco and many other brand campaigns, the advertising has given the organization an identity, a status – and in 'Be The Best' even an inspiring slogan – to unite behind, and something that serving personnel can be proud of.

Most importantly, though, the campaign has played a significant part in beginning to change perceptions of the Army among the public as a whole. While these people may not even have a direct effect on potential recruits in the way that friends, parents and teachers might, public perception filters through into every part of the brand context. This is a valid and important objective for the advertising, and one that will increasingly be seen in equivalent campaigns for other organizations. Take for instance the police's 'Could You?' campaign, or 'Those who can, teach'.

Few organizations have the requirement for such high-profile recruitment campaigns, but the lessons to be learned from the Army are more to do with how many aspects of brand communication can be used to demonstrate – often in the most credible manner – a brand's intentions by how it acts, and with the effects of these intentions being communicated to a wider audience than the primary target. While recruitment advertising continues to be a low-interest area, often totally divorced from the marketing department, it will continue to run the risk of undermining the brand. And of course, this process neatly links into our previous example when the recruits become employees, and start to deliver the brand vision. The successor to recruitment advertising, internal communications, is often even more woefully overlooked. Organizations that can involve their employees and give them a degree of ownership over the external brand messages can expect better delivery of that message. To quote Colin Mitchell (2002):

> By applying many of the principles of consumer advertising to internal communications, leaders can guide employees to a better understanding of, and even a passion for, the brand vision. ...customers are much more likely to experience the company in a way that's consistent with what you've promised.

PLANNING IN THE NEW BRAND CONTEXT

What I hope to demonstrate with these examples is how some brands and sectors use brand communications to communicate beyond the traditional relationship of brand and potential customer. In some cases, most obviously recruitment advertising, brands have always communicated to people who are not 'customers' in the strictest sense. But the intention of looking at these examples is to learn lessons that can be applied to any brand, because planning and managing brands in the new brand context involves taking account of many audiences beyond customers themselves, and the remainder of the chapter seeks to identify some areas to consider. None of these areas requires new planning skills or techniques, and certainly not a massive change in approach; what most entail is a wider breadth of approach and consideration.

Holistic brand planning

The most significant observation from the new brand context is how multi-faceted brands now are. Brands need to communicate with so many different audiences precisely because people are aware of those audiences and are able to access the brand through so many different points. At first sight, this could sound as if planning brand communications in such a complicated context could be an impossible task. I would certainly agree that planning brands is harder in this new context than it was in the days when brands had a simple 'parent–child' relationship with their customers. Sadly, a common theme is still for advertising agency planners to feel that other parts of the brand and its points of contact are somehow less interesting and beneath them.

However, the planning department's response to the new context should be to rise to the challenge, because rather than purely planning brand communications, brand planners should now be taking responsibility for all aspects of the brand: wherever and however the brand makes contact with the outside world is as relevant a part of the planner's remit as the 60-second television spot. It is easier to pay lip-service to this notion than to implement it, as it requires a commitment to the brand from every part of the organization, not just the marketing department. In effect, it requires every part of the organization to feel themselves managers of their part of the brand; by the same token, it demands that brand objectives that would traditionally have meant a communications brief may entail a response from any part of the organization – from distribution, to uniforms, to product development.

Suddenly planning the brand becomes very close to running the organization: brand planners will need to learn a very wide set of skills to do a successful job and carry the rest of the organization with them, and their agencies will need to offer a far wider set of services than the strictly defined advertising/promotion/PR/DM disciplines of the past. See the Revised Millennium Definition of Account Planning on the APG Web site, offered by our own co-editor Merry Baskin.

The power of tweaking

I don't suppose the governments I referred to earlier see themselves as completely hamstrung; they have adapted to making policy that 'tweaks' economic conditions, and they know that getting a set of relatively minor micro-economic factors right can reap enormous rewards. So too is the case with brand management: the forces outside the brand's direct control are not necessarily evil, and the astute brand strategy will increasingly use them to its advantage. The wonderful and not heard often enough concept of 'judo marketing' seeks to do exactly this: to 'tweak' the brand into a position where the momentum of habit or opinion works in its favour.

For instance, understanding in detail what public opinion consists of and where it comes from can allow a brand to target the sources of those opinions; knowing and understanding where the strength of opinion lies allows a brand to position itself in line with that opinion. As there are more sources of information and points of contact with a brand, so brand managers have more channels of communication to exploit. Understanding the strengths and weaknesses of the brand at each of these points of contact is a key skill for any brand planner. While customers might expect complete consistency at all points, few brands can deliver it in reality; the clever communications strategy will take account of this and attempt to 'tweak' only the ones that can (and need to) be addressed. With increasing remit and reducing budgets, knowing how to prioritize and play to a brand's strengths is increasingly important.

Planning fights its way upstream

Ever since some management consultant (presumably) coined the phrase 'upstream thinking', every professional discipline has set itself the objective of playing in the pure intellectual water of the upstream pond. In conventional wisdom, as long as brand planning concentrates on communications, it should inevitably find itself further down the process, and run the risk of losing its role as champion of the brand. But in the new brand context, organizations need to understand that every part of the business is in the business of communicating – maybe not directly with customers, but with other elements that affect the brand. If this communication is going to be directed, and add up to coherence at its various points of contact, it has to be directed (and planned) from the top.

This is a task that marketing people alone cannot achieve: as our examples have shown, communicating beyond the traditional brand–customer relationship requires commitment from all parts of the brand's organization, and managing the brand has to be a core part of the organization's commercial strategy. While the CEO may not wish to assume day-to-day responsibilities as brand planner in chief, that is effectively part of his or her role, as any of the organization's actions will affect perceptions of its brands. For most brand planners, this implication will not in practice mean an automatic seat at the legendary 'top table', but a requirement to devise and implement brand strategies that are effected upwards and outwards through the organization, not just downwards through the marketing department and its agencies.

Stay flexible, get real

I have made much of how many different aspects of the brand people are likely to see, and how many different places they are likely to meet it. And, yes, people do expect consistency wherever they come across it; but consistent does not mean identical. The conventional wisdom in brand marketing is, of course, that consumers should see the same thing wherever they encounter the brand. Increasingly, though, with deeper understanding of what brands are and how they work, people also appreciate that a brand may have several faces, and behave differently in different situations; the problems only start occurring when these different faces are inconsistent. Obvious examples are communications in different media: no-one expects or demands detailed product or price information in television ads, which are recognized as brand-building awareness tools; in sectors where price is a regular aspect of communications, people expect a brand to have at least a different tone of voice. Airlines are a fine example: the same airline can speak (and, indeed, behave) with a different attitude when it is talking with its business, economy or even low-cost hat on, just as the same customer might travel Club on business, World Traveller on holiday or Go for a weekend away, and bring different decision-making criteria each time.

One consequence of both brands and customers wearing different hats is that one can often find quite different interpretations of the same piece of communication, and here one finds the implications for brand planning. Rather than expecting identical perceptions and identical responses we must learn to accept a wider range of experiences of the brand, and consequently a wider range of perceptions. Rather than planning for, and attempting to evaluate on, an identical set of perceptions and understanding, we now have to dig deeper to understand the consistencies (or otherwise) and synergy or dissonance between all the brand's various manifestations, and often between different audiences' reactions to the same piece of communication.

Do as they do, not as they say

It is true that most people are more informed about brands and brand communications, and these communications now address even more informed audiences. The result is that brand planners and researchers spend more of their time talking to and listening to people who know they are better informed, and sound as if they know what they are talking about. The temptation is to take their comments at face value, or at least to give them more credence because of their position of greater knowledge.

This can be even more dangerous than letting customers write your ads: audiences such as these are more involved with the brand, but they also have their own agendas, and quite often their own slant on a situation which is just as coloured by their own context. Quite simply, when planning communications against these audiences there is no easy short-cut: no matter how eloquently they can tell you what to do, the same disciplines of research, analysis, planning and evaluation apply. The difference is that many of these disciplines – research and evaluation in particular – are made harder by dealing with an audience that is more likely to be telling you what it wants you to hear than what it actually thinks. But that is a topic for another book – or, indeed, other chapters in this one.

A FINAL EXHORTATION

To sum up, these implications really just scratch the surface of how the role of brand planning and brand management is changing. If the world is becoming more complex, then the world of brands is doing so even faster. But there is one theme running through all of these issues, and that is the need for planning in particular to understand its brands and their many audiences even more thoroughly than before, and to treat them as changing, dynamic concepts that can be enhanced by their context. To me, that makes brand planning sound a great deal more interesting and fun than the one-way communications of the past.

REFERENCES

Baskin, M, Revised Millennium Definition of Account Planning, [Online] www.apg.org.uk

Cowley, D (ed) (1991/1996) *Understanding Brands: By 10 people who do*, Kogan Page

IPA (2000) *How 'Every Little Helps' Was a Big Help to Tesco*, IPA Effectiveness Awards

Klein, N (2001) *No Logo*, Flamingo

Mitchell, C (2002) Selling the brand inside, *Harvard Business Review*, January

Chapter 5

Brand strategy versus brand tactics: tinker, tailor, soldier, sailor – why strategy should be flexible but tactics are important

John Cronk

John Cronk, 40, started his career in qualitative research, before moving to Still Price Court Twivy D'Souza – an agency that marked the high point of silly names and offered obvious career possibilities for someone named Cronk. He then started Navigator, a qualitative research and planning consultancy. After a few years of this he was struck down with a surprisingly

common yet life-threatening ailment called 'wanting to be in the film business' and started a dual film production and marketing strategy business. This succeeded well in that any money made through strategy work was immediately used up by the film stuff.

He co-founded Mangiare Restaurants in 2000 and currently divides his time between being Marketing Director (or Head of Leaflets) of Mangiare and being a freelance researcher and planner. He goes yacht racing when he can find the time.

INTRODUCTION

By the 1970s the notion of strategy as the key to potent marketing and planning was becoming well accepted, and it now passes without question. We tend to use 'strategy' or 'planning' to mean having a plan that involves a defined target audience, a clearly stated proposition, and focusing the entire advertising or marketing thrust against these two objects.

The availability of increasingly detailed quantitative market data and the advent of qualitative research to help understand consumer motivations, needs and reactions has also helped to create the idea that in any given situation there is a strategic 'blueprint for success' lurking somewhere. At the same time, 'tactical' activity has become thoroughly devalued: it is now a dirty word used to define smaller or less fundamentally relevant marketing activity, and is often considered to be actively detrimental to the brand in question.

This has tended to lead to the search for a kind of 'Grand Strategy'; the planning Big Idea which, if thought through with sufficient thoroughness and executed with vigour, will win the day. The Grand Plan is also characteristically the product of military thinking or a military metaphor. This is hugely seductive, but equally deceptive. Unfortunately in real life the Grand Plan is inevitably flawed (or the information upon which it is based is flawed) and such a plan intrinsically is limited in its ability to react to changing circumstances. In real life the result of this kind of battle-plan thinking in a marketing context is often more like the grinding stalemate of the Battle of the Somme rather than the stunning success of the Blitzkrieg.

But why should military metaphors have exclusive rights? Aren't there other activities closer to home that might lead us to a more balanced view of strategy and tactics? Yacht racing, of which I have some experience, did not strike me immediately as being of any relevance to marketing. But on further reflection a number of potentially useful parallels emerge.

Yacht racing involves a great deal of science. It requires knowledge of aerodynamics, fluid dynamics, structural engineering and a vast array of other technical competencies – but its greatest exponents are those who know that understanding the science is merely a prerequisite to the creative thinking, 'the art', that divides the winners from the rest. Similarly, marketing is both a science and art, and those who put their faith in it being only one or the other will generally fail.

A yacht race has no defined track – just a featureless expanse of sea. A yacht-racing course consists of a number of buoys, which must be rounded in a certain sequence. In a long race these buoys can be many miles away, well out of sight. The competitive environment is thus defined primarily by the relative position of your competitors.

The truth about modern markets is that they too are an environment defined solely by the position of the competitors, rather than by any absolute geography. There is no such thing as a 'market' in any physical sense. No longer can the consumer go to a place where the competing vendors are gathered, shouting their offers. The market, as an effect of the fragmentation of both communication and distribution channels, is anywhere and everywhere. And often even the product has no physical existence. This vision of the market clearly suggests that it is highly likely to change and that it must be best to keep thinking as you go. And if that seems tactical rather than strategic, well, it's what winners do.

MARKET RESEARCH IS LIKE THE WEATHER FORECAST: YOU'VE GOT TO TAKE IT INTO ACCOUNT, BUT YOU CAN'T TRUST IT

Market research is one obvious way in which we try to get a grip on the shape of the market, just as the weather forecast is one way we try to get a grip on the likely 'geography' of a yacht race. The weather forecast is useful, but it won't tell you how to win the race. It can occasionally be very inaccurate and is only ever a guide to likely conditions. Your competitors probably have the same information.

Exactly the same limitations apply to market research as to weather forecasts. We should treat all qualitative and quantitative information in the same way in terms of its predictive ability. The lesson is that, although we should have a point of view, we need to be prepared to deal with times when things are not to be as we thought they would be.

It is a yacht-racing truism that the conditions at any major regatta will generally be atypical for that area. The locals' plea that 'it isn't usually like this round here' is a standing joke.

DON'T BE TIED DOWN BY A STRATEGY: USE A 'STARTEGY'

Anyone who claims to have sailed a successful race while adhering totally to a prearranged plan is a liar. The same probably applies in marketing. Conditions change. Your strategy should have the ability to change, or rather you should have the mental flexibility to develop it. Assessment of your strategy should be a continuous process, rather than, as is so often the case, something to be done after it shows signs of failing. Think of your strategy as a starting point, as a 'startegy', a plan that seems like the best idea given current knowledge, but a plan that is under review from the moment you decide on it.

I find that this approach also has the advantage of allowing me to spot the effects of my own incompetence as early as possible. Useful in yacht racing, vital in marketing.

FORTUNE FAVOURS THE BOLD: IF YOU GO WHERE OTHERS ARE AFRAID TO GO, YOU MAY BEAT THEM

There may be some absolute no-go areas in a yacht race – dry land being the example that springs to mind most readily. Perhaps land is equivalent to the various commonly agreed constraints that we find in a marketing context. Price, product function and morality can all be seen as creating absolute no-go areas. However, in yacht racing there is often advantage to be gained by being close to the dangerous bits. There are fewer competitors to be found there and generally the more space you have to yourself, the clearer your wind and the faster you go.

> I have won races by going close to the beach. I have lost races by going aground. It's the ratio that matters.

KNOWING THE REAL RISK

There is no such thing as a risk-free strategy, but it is important to try to understand what is actually at risk. In reality the land meets the sea in awkward and unpredictable shallow bits. Sometimes these have soft mud on the bottom and so the penalty for going too close is going aground, which is slow but not fatal. In other areas the shallows are rocky, which implies the possibility of sinking and so a greater real risk. On a sandy or muddy coast you can sail along with a few inches of water under the keel using your echo sounder; on a rocky shore you may need to allow 10 feet. The severity of the downside of the risk is as important as the level of risk itself. So it's a further element to be factored into the strategy – which is increasingly, and I think inevitably, presenting itself as an informed gamble.

> I was once racing across a large bay near Cowes where I sailed dinghies in my teens. I knew that there is one largish rock somewhere near the middle, couldn't be sure where exactly, but it would be really bad luck to hit it. As it happened we did hit it and I was reminded that the effect on a light dinghy or on a boat weighing a couple of tons is remarkably similar. One stops with a huge bang as the keel nearly tears off and almost immediately one starts thinking about the hideous cost of boat repairs.

KNOWING WHERE YOU ARE DOESN'T TELL YOU WHICH WAY TO GO

Knowing where you are is perhaps the most important piece of information in both yacht racing and marketing, but on its own it is useless. Knowing where you are doesn't imply that you necessarily know where you should be heading. Endless data can be reassuring – until you need to decide what to actually do.

> As an inexperienced navigator I used to spend a huge amount of time checking and re-checking the boat's position. This left very little time to think about where we should be heading. We tended not to do very well.

LEADERS LEAD, FOLLOWERS LOSE

On the few occasions that I have won a race, or even held the lead for a while, I have been struck by the fact that being out in front is really gruelling. It is really hard to be the leader in a yacht race. Remember, there's no visible track to the finish. It's mentally far easier to be number two or three, doing well, but seemingly without the big decisions to make. But leading is the only place to be if you want to win. In planning, being a number two or three brand, with a strategy that is only marginally differentiated from that of the leader, can be a comfortable place to be – but it means being a loser in the end.

> About 10 hours into a race round the Isle of Wight we found ourselves in second place to a boat whose skipper had been a member of the German Admirals Cup team in the 1980s. Our boat was about a hundred yards behind, and had been for the last three hours. He was an excellent sailor and in chasing him we'd raised our game so that we both had a huge lead on the rest of the fleet. The course took us against the current and the obvious move was to go inshore. We went a little further inshore than the other boat and over the next half hour we overtook it. After all that time the shock nearly killed me. My concentration collapsed and I was almost looking for a reason to hand back the lead. We thought we weren't winners and he was. A bit of role reversal had one of the crew giving me a pep talk, and we held them off all the way to the finish.

CHECK WHERE THE OPPOSITION IS, BUT KEEP LOOKING AHEAD

When you're in the lead you need to look ahead, not behind. Becoming fascinated by what the boats behind are doing generally means that you will shortly join them. On the other hand, have a look regularly to check that they're not catching up, and if they are, set someone else to work out why, while the rest of you get on with sailing your own boat fast.

TAKE EVERY OPPORTUNITY TO DUMP ON THE OPPOSITION

Sailing in the backwash of another boat is slow. If you are in front, subject to keeping going in the desired direction, you position yourself to dump on those behind. If you are behind you try to get into clear air – you are never going to catch up otherwise. So when you are behind, you zig when they zag. Easier said than done in sailing, and easier said than done in marketing, but equally vital.

Many people know that Ben Ainslie won his Gold medal at the 2000 Olympics by sailing his only rival down into 22nd place in the final race. He broke no rules to do so, but utilized an initial advantage to destroy his opponent. (Fewer people know that four years earlier the same opponent had done exactly the same to him. Learning from other people's strategies is a good thing too.)

A FAST BOAT MAKES YOU LOOK LIKE A GREAT STRATEGIST; A GREAT AD MAKES YOU LOOK LIKE A GREAT PLANNER

Basically, if you're the person on a yacht calling the shots, deciding where the boat goes, you're like the planner in an agency team. The person steering is akin to the creative. If he or she does a really good job you look good too. Sadly, vice versa doesn't work well. A slow boat is a slow boat even if it's going the right way, and a crap ad with a great strategy is still a crap ad. The lesson here is again that planning does not end with the production of the brief. It is vital to stay involved in the process of execution, to stay in touch with the creatives.

I've lost races in fast boats and I've lost races in slow boats, but I've never won a race in a slow boat.

CHANGING CONDITIONS MEAN OPPORTUNITIES FOR GAIN

In yacht racing the corners are where it all happens. Changes in direction are dictated at the turning marks – but what should the course be? When markets change or when a leading brand changes strategy is when it all happens. Again, the pressure on the leader is huge, but it has to take a view. The following boats are watching to see how it pans out before finalizing their own plans. Indecision is fatal.

NOT ALL SITUATIONS OFFER THE POTENTIAL FOR DRAMATIC GAINS

In fact most situations don't. Stick with the fleet until you find a real opportunity. A lot of yacht races are won by the boat that made the least mistakes rather than the cleverest moves. Remember that if it's obviously a good idea everyone will do it; if it isn't obvious, it has risk attached. When there is no opportunity for a masterstroke, work on the detail: it can add up to a gain. On a boat this means trimming the sails for best speed, moving crew around for optimum trim and focusing on simply sailing fast. In marketing it means a myriad of things, from POS to media efficiency, but if done well they can add up to a gain. While this is going on make sure someone is thinking about possibilities for a masterstroke on the next leg of the race. This is called 'keeping your head out of the boat' and is a good excuse for navigator/tacticians not to do any manual labour. Planners may feel the same way about it.

> As novices in the 1991 Fastnet race we didn't have much of a strategy, apart from trying hard all the time. Unusually, we had two navigators on board and for five days we simply kept the boat pointing precisely towards the next mark and then the finish line. We did OK.

DON'T GIVE UP EASILY

Sometimes you try something and it doesn't work. Stay in the race, don't go home and sack the crew. (Is there a lesson for agency and client relationships here?)

One of the most refreshing things I have heard recently was Rupert Howell talking about one of HHCL's longstanding clients. He said, 'The first campaign we did for them didn't work.'

Finally, some key differences between marketing and yacht racing. If you do something dramatically different from the fleet in a yacht race and you're wrong you end up last. If you do something different in marketing, usually nothing much happens. I'm always surprised how worried people are by the potential downside, as in my experience a campaign that turns out to be a damp squib is just that, it doesn't go bang. Maybe the kind of strategies I'm often involved in are simply not that radical. Which relates to the other key difference. A yacht race has a start and a finish. Marketing a brand doesn't. Barring catastrophes, you get a chance to try again.

Chapter 6

Time to let go

Peter Wells and Tim Hollins

Peter Wells is the founder of nilewide, whose aim is simply to move our thinking about marketing along just one step further each week, through critically reviewing and analysing the latest thinking from around the world. He is a relentless traveller, and after a career in international marketing on four continents, nilewide provided the perfect opportunity to explore and challenge our most fundamental thinking, and to provide a channel for the ideas of so many people from around the world. Peter is just one of the voices for those ideas, through a variety of media and for clients in the UK, USA, Europe, Africa and Australia. www.nilewide.com

Tim Hollins is a founding partner of the international brand development consultancy Headmint, based in London and New York. Headmint is unique in its specialization in the process of strategy development, creating and customizing strategy products in order to help multi-disciplined client teams build their brands from inside the business. Current clients include Coca-Cola, British Telecom, Ford, Nestlé, Ralph Lauren, Scottish and Newcastle and Y&R worldwide.

Tim lives in a small cottage by the sea in Sussex, England. When at home, he enjoys cycling, the seaside and imagining what his kitchen could be like if he got rid of the one from the mid-1970s.

Tim and Headmint can be contacted through their Web site Headmint.com

My father and his mates may not be the obvious place to start when it comes to new brand thinking, but this is a good place. Not because they created the brand thinking of the new century, but because the massive changes they experienced in their lifetimes make me wonder whether we really are in the business of new brand thinking.

Unfortunately it appears that much of our brand thinking is still constrained by the rules and illusions about marketing that were set when Dad came back from the war. Illusions that are set in the ethos of control and hierarchy that dominated the post-war boom. To those of you who disagree, I hope this at least encourages some new thinking.

DAD AND HIS MATES

Yes, my old man did rule our house with an iron fist. He ruled the dining table, for compulsory Sunday lunches, in much the same way as his generation ran their companies. They took the mores of their time, combined with the rules they learnt in the life-changing events of the war, to run their lives, their wives and their businesses. And naturally this had a strong control element. They were in charge and wanted to control what was going on.

This applied to marketing as well and it was the time that gave rise to the 'marketing concept'. It was a time when many companies were selling stuff to people who didn't have all the stuff they wanted. Which I am sure sounds like a pretty cool job to many people today, who are stuck with multiple undifferentiated competitors all competing on price and seeing who can yell the loudest.

That things are different today only reflects the changes that my father experienced in the last 40 years of his life. In a nutshell, our social history went something like this. By the time I grew up in the 1960s and 1970s the social control structures were already changing. We started out suburban kids, but soon the peace lovers fought with police, smoked drugs and grew their hair. Advertisers spoke to people who were growing richer than ever and looking to buy. Then I grew my hair and discovered the surf. My brother cut his and became a lawyer (go figure). My father still controlled the dining table, yet the conflict increased and the facade of control slipped every now and then.

My marriage came and went, yet Amex tells me they still want something like one! My daughter grew up, checking the surf (an Aussie beach babe). Now she fights with her mother and treats my place like a hotel. Sometimes she feels life is out of control. She goes from one thing to the next, never stays still and decides who is cool today. She wears Porn Star and Just Stop It. She's in a chat room, on the phone and listening to the radio at the same time. I have no control over her. We collide, connect and meld in our relationship. She collides with thousands of others; sometimes they connect. She knows what she likes and won't be told.

THE POINT OF THIS PERSONAL STORY

The point is, in just a short time our societies have changed enormously. This potted personal story is just one view, and many will argue with it and include many other dramatic events. I am happy with that because it only reinforces the point.

I want to use it to focus on the issue of control. As the story demonstrates, control structures in our societies have changed dramatically. This is of course true in business, and we have seen considerable data showing the loss of trust in traditional institutions, from government to corporations, as well as endless rhetoric about how the power has shifted to consumers. All of course is supported by data such as the baby boomers being the richest generation the world has seen, growing wealth due to rising share and real estate markets, greater flows of information and ease of communication through technology, and many markets becoming commodity markets.[1] But there are no real new ideas here.

MATURITY

So life has changed and so have markets. But what about marketing? Sometimes it appears that marketing is not maturing, too often it appears to cling to its past in a way that leads it to do things so that it at least feels like it is still in control. It clings to the old in the hope that it can hold off the inevitable. In a weird kind of way, it is acting like my old man and his mates in the way they naturally, and lovingly, tried to hold onto what they knew and cherished.

That of course is fair enough, but we need to ask: is marketing as a discipline at the end of its life, mature and with wisdom to pass on in a changing world, or is it still just a child with a lifetime in which to grow and mature? My answer is that it is probably a teenager, while no doubt many others, including Mark Earls in his other book, *Welcome to the Creative Age*, may argue it is at the end of its life. Perhaps it doesn't really matter; what does matter is that we had better think far more clearly about what we are doing and whether we are just trying to hold on to the past because that is what we know and are comfortable with.

THE FATHER KOTLER

One of the things that we are struggling to hold on to is the idea that marketers are in control of marketing, something we can probably blame the old man and his mates for. Classical marketing theory is based on a belief that marketing is in control. The eminent Professor Kotler's view was that marketing is analysis, planning, implementation and measurement: a perspective that supports, encourages and may even be the basis of this belief. But if that is not a good enough example of marketing's love of feeling in control, let's consider positioning theory and its common practice as understanding where a brand fits on a matrix and then suggesting how it can be moved to a more beneficial position.

A little honesty will suggest that, no matter whether we are marketers, consultants, researchers, planners or just wishful thinkers, we have all at some stage put a brand in one quadrant of a matrix and announced with confidence that we can move it up and to the right (why is it never down to the left?). By implication this is something that marketers can do and control, even if it ignores the fact that we have little control (a major understatement) over how competitors, customers and potential customers may react.

Somehow we have created illusions about how much control we really have. Of course this is for a good reason: we want to keep our jobs.

TALKING OF CONTROL

Just as we have created illusions of control, we have also created a language of marketing that reinforces theses illusions. UK research leader,

Wendy Gordon, has pointed out that even the most common phrases, such as target market, are control oriented. These expressions give an impression that people are static and we can line them up and take some sort of action to make them like a brand.[2] This language reinforces the illusions of control.

THE CLINTON FACTOR

Being in control is a symbol of power, and people who appear to lack control are often viewed negatively, be it in business, on the sporting field or in their personal lives. Organizations have been structured to maintain power through control: for example, the classical hierarchical organization is a means for a few to control larger numbers of people and their activities. In politics control has been a key issue for all governments, from dictatorships to the democratically elected, and is exerted through the media, bureaucracies and legislation. Of course it is no surprise that people misuse their control and power, or that it has a seductive appeal to those who think they lack it. This is of course understandable and logical if we are to avoid the implications of chaos. Or in the case of business if it is also to grow and prosper.

IT AIN'T THE SAME NO MORE

But the world is changing, and there are signs of a move away from acceptance of the established ideas of corporate control and power, graphically demonstrated by the anti-globalization movement. This movement involves many groups, and at its heart is concern over how a few can exert control over many. Particularly, how an undemocratically elected few can do this, recognizing that companies are undemocratic institutions given permission to operate in democratic societies, and that one dollar per vote in the market is different from one person per vote in a democracy.[3]

The protests were the violent, confronting face of concerns about corporate control and individuals having no control over a situation. These concerns are seen in a host of political spheres and in various ways in different countries. This review will raise some that are more applicable to marketing.

Young people, and the shift from them having little control to becoming influential, are another powerful example of how there is an irrepressible move away from the old control orientations. No longer are children seen and not heard, no longer are teenagers supposed to be controlled by families and schools, in Western culture at least. Each has been given the right to control some aspects of their own lives, presumably with a corresponding decrease in absolute control for parents, particularly fathers.

This breakdown of control structures is recognized in postmodernism and is increasingly accepted. Trust in traditional controlling institutions, such as governments, churches, schools and corporations, is breaking down.[4] People are now questioning the idea that others can exert control over them, or perhaps more commonly, they as individuals do not accept that they have no control. We now feel we can dip into cultures and momentarily take the things we like, that we no longer have to conform to the dictates of others when it comes to many aspects of our lives, from clothes to music.

MARKETING'S FADING LIGHT

With these changes, we should probably expect that the old control orientations so beloved by marketing theory's originators may not be as effective as they once were. And so it should be no surprise that marketing's traditional tools seem to be less and less effective, despite the overwhelming interest in effectiveness. Despite the plethora of effectiveness awards in big budget areas such as advertising, there is rising ad avoidance, media inflation, increasing numbers of ads and a growing anti-brand movement that complains about ad invasions into private and public spaces.[5]

No doubt this obsession with effectiveness awards is part of the inherent desire to prove we are in control of what we are doing, and as our tools become less effective, our desire to prove them increases. Of course effectiveness awards are important, but they need to prove an effectiveness outcome that matters, simply ROI, because no matter how many other things we measure to prove we are doing something right, it is ultimately about returns on investment. More on this to come.

Newer tools also seem to be struggling, and may even have a shorter life. For example, there is already growing concern over the way marketing uses data and manipulates so-called relationships. The most devastating research comes from the UK, where only 9 per cent of consumers were happy with companies driving, or controlling, contact with them.[6]

Even in the increasingly popular areas of word of mouth, both in the physical world and online, in the form of viral marketing and idea viruses, there is a desire to control.[7] It is seen in many of the questions put to Malcolm Gladwell, author of *The Tipping Point*, about how we can control what people talk about.[8] Yet at the same time, there is the frightening realization that viral marketing opens channels for positive and negative flows of information.[9]

LIVING IN AN ILLUSION

This discussion suggests that many of the things we do are done to create an illusion of control. So desperately do we want to hang on to these illusions, it seems we are prepared to ignore the limitations in the thinking behind marketing strategy.

A starting point is seeing that many of the basics of marketing are embedded in the past. This is something we all know, but why do we fail to acknowledge that extrapolating them to the present and future is dangerous? Every day we do this, with the most obvious being in marketing research and concepts such as brand heritage, which are in fact based on a reality in the past. To extrapolate them to the present, we are prepared to ignore that people are constantly changing, which conflicts with a postmodern perspective.[2]

Accepting that people are constantly changing means that marketing does not have as much control over its effectiveness as it may believe. This should lead to more critical consideration of whether other common practices are creating illusions of control. Some areas that should be questioned include fundamental issues, such as whether marketers really create brands or they do so in combination with buyers, what is persuasion and what is its relevance, can we really have relationships without personal contact, and do people really want something akin to a human relationship with something that is not human?

ILLUSIONS BECOME SELF-DECEPTION

This questioning embraces the views of a number of commentators who ask why we do not acknowledge that marketing is also done by the buyer.[10] The general view is that marketing is something that marketers do, but the reality is that buyers have always done marketing. They have sought information, evaluated it and actively discussed brands, although not always positively. The interest in word of mouth only reinforces the fact that buyers are doing marketing as well.

In essence we are deceiving ourselves into the belief that it is what marketers do that is important. The reality is that it is what both marketers and buyers do that ultimately brings success. Marketing is not just something that marketers do: they are contributors to it, but do not control it. This thinking sets new challenges for marketing theory development and practice.

BRANDS ARE CO-CREATED

One outcome of accepting that both marketers and buyers do marketing is that brands are co-created by the seller and customer.[11] Both parties contribute value to a brand; the seller cannot just tell or persuade someone what a brand is. Instead the brand owner can set the preconditions for what the two parties may create.

The very idea that marketers create brands needs to be challenged. Even the basic belief that marketers create the brand's personality is shaky, as research shows that buyers ascribe their own desired personality traits to the brands they use. People who don't use the brand tend not to ascribe personality traits to the brand.[12] Sure marketers can play a role, but it is the buyer who ascribes personality traits, and at best brand personality is co-created.

Of course, co-creation does not mean that both parties have to contribute equally or at all; what is required is the ability for both to contribute. This can be seen in packaged goods, where buyers may want nothing more than the option to contribute. For many people, most packaged goods are low involvement and they have no interest in contributing to the brand, any more than just habitually buying when the brand is on the shelf. Relating this to theories such as Robert Heath's low involvement processing of advertising, it simply acknowledges that the level of co-creation may go no deeper than having some memory of the brand name.[13]

At the same time, it accepts that there are brands that are important to people, though this will never be more than very few for each person.[14] These may be recognized as those few brands that someone will go elsewhere to buy if the brand is not on the shelf. They probably also include brands people use to create their own self-identity, such as certain fashion labels.

LEARNING FROM OTHERS

Co-creating brands in different ways is fraught with concerns, because it challenges the way we think about investment and risk in marketing. Therefore it may be interesting to look for lessons from outside marketing and business. Film director Oliver Stone suggests communication involves 'telling and not telling', and talks of older actors who knew 'how to withhold'. This is the important recognition that what is not said, done or shown, is just as important as what is. In the context of storytelling and communications, this not telling or withholding leaves gaps for viewers to create their own meaning, rather than the storyteller dictating meaning. This leaving of gaps can also be seen in films from different cultures. For example, Hollywood blockbusters often leave no gaps for the viewer, and hence are entertaining, but leave a shallow feeling afterwards, while French cinema leaves wider gaps, and some films never close them, leaving much of the meaning up to the viewer.[15]

This can also be seen in that all too common feeling of 'I loved the book, but didn't like the movie; [the star] was nothing like I envisaged [the main character].' What has happened is that the novelist can allow readers to co-create their own meaning, while some film adaptations try to force it on to the viewer, leaving no room for the individual to create meaning.

Another way to view this is through the difference between leadership and dictatorship. Great leaders set the preconditions for people to go on to co-create greatness. In business they set values and visions that allow people to make mistakes, take risks and work together towards a vision that is not constrained by telling people what to think. Dictatorship tries to tell people what to think and force them to behave in one way, leaving little room for co-creating. In other words dictatorship is about control, while leadership accepts that we cannot control everything; it allows others to have some control.

The lack of control is also recognized in many other varied activities, for instance in high performance motor cycle riding. Doug Chandler, a former world champion, points out that the first reaction to entering a corner too quickly is to pull hard on the brakes, but this almost inevitably leads to failure and a crash. Instead the rider needs to allow the motorcycle to do what it does, which is to remain stable when it is accelerating through a corner; in other words to give control over to the motorcycle at that point. Similar situations exist in many sports: for example, anyone who has snow skied knows that an attempt to exert control over one's skis on the ice will lead to a painful crash. Instead you need to let the skis do what they do, turn slowly and consistently, and wait until the conditions and the skis are in the right position to turn more dramatically.

FROM CONTROL TO ACCEPTING

Clearly, giving up control is difficult and even painful. This is why we pursue illusions of control, and it is why some religions address the fallacy of trying to pursue control. Buddhism recognizes it as a fundamental trait, although it points out that it is also impossible to achieve. (That the major Western religions mandate what is right and ethical, or seek to control ethical behaviour, may be one of the reasons why control is so ingrained in the Western psyche). Philosophers such as Nietzsche have also discussed this desire for control and power and highlighted its foolishness.

No one likes the feeling of not being in control, but recognizing that we are not in control can open up new possibilities and a better perspective.

SO TO CONTROLLING OUR BRANDS

Today we are only just beginning to think about how we can co-create brands that benefit both buyers and sellers without resorting to the old ways of control as espoused by classical marketing theory. One starting point may be to think about what we can influence and in turn where we can only create the preconditions for people to co-create/co-market with marketers. Gary Hamel focuses on preconditions for strategy to emerge, rather than suggesting we can force it to emerge, and this may be a useful way to think of many marketing activities. Preconditions focuses attention on what can and cannot be influenced, and on acceptance that you cannot control or force the outcome.[16]

Applying this perspective to brands supports the increasingly common view that brands are about corporate culture and reside within companies. What happens within companies is something that marketers have more control over than do the thoughts and actions of people outside the company. This also recognizes that if marketers are to have an influence it will be over their own inputs into what is co-created, not how someone else sees them or contributes. Perhaps we may finally acknowledge that any two people will make sense of the same thing in different ways, because they are two different people with different histories, genetics and viewpoints.[17]

For many people the scariest implication of this view is that the aspect of marketing we have least control over is communications, yet this is also the area where we want to have control, because of the cost. Advertising is the classic example of this, and there is still a great belief in the importance of persuasion, something Andrew Ehrenberg describes as a romantic ideal.[18]

LETTING GO

Based on this thinking, there is no escaping the idea that marketers must be prepared to let go of their brands, or at least, parts of their brands. This is no small issue as they are investing significant amounts in 'creating' or 'building' brands. It also runs head on into the belief that companies create and therefore own brands, and can account for them on their balance sheets. The implications of this are significant, given the way companies are valued, legislation in many countries and the workings of the stock market.

Despite the fear and difficulties, some marketers have recognized that they are not in control and there are many ways in which brands are being co-created. The starting point is to address what can be controlled, which is generally only something that is inside the organization. This is seen in the growing emphasis on organizational culture and its role in ensuring success.[19] While organizational culture cannot be controlled – it is co-created by everyone – it is an area that can be influenced and made explicit by managers. By understanding what can and cannot be controlled, the company should have a clearer view of where it can and cannot go.

There are many ways in which we can concentrate on what we can control and let go of other areas. It may be as simple as recognizing that communication tends to be a monologue that leaves little room for the recipient to create any meaning, of course recognizing that it is up to people to decide if they wish to create meaning. Even if they don't want to, low involvement processing theory suggests people will still lay down some memories and may use them at a later date. Therefore the brand associations need to be seen as a platform to be used at a later date.

If we believe there will be conscious processing of a communication, then we should also consider whether we really should use our old control-oriented feature, attribute and benefit processes to design communications that leave no room for any misinterpretation and that, at their best, may persuade. Instead we can set the preconditions for individuals to reach a conclusion themselves; they may even come to more relevant benefits or attributes for themselves. But of course, talk to creative people and they say it's about viewers, listeners or people creating their own benefits, not trying to hit them on the head with one. Somewhere we have lost this idea when it comes to the processes of marketing.

If we have a more expansive view we can probably see that it is not what we say in a communication that really matters at all. But it is what people say about a brand that is really important. Ah, but we can't control that, so we create an illusion or romantic ideal of persuasion. If we accept that what is said in the ad is part of creating a platform for people to think and talk about a brand, then new vistas open. Nothing new in this, but why do we fail to really commit to it?

Communication is only one way we can think about how we set the platform for people to co-create the brand.

PEOPLE ARE THE PRODUCT

Some preliminary thinking suggests there are a multitude of ways a brand can be co-created by the seller and buyer. At its extreme, the seller simply provides the framework for buyers to join together to create the brand. Examples include Ebay, where people provide the items that create the market and buy them, while Zagat is a brand created by the input of diners to recommend restaurants. Popular television programmes, such as *Survivor* and *Big Brother* in the UK, are also examples of people being the product, as people apply to join and then vote for the individuals to stay or go.

PEOPLE CHANGE ITS USE

Another way that buyers co-create is when they use a product for their own purposes. For example, Apple allows people to co-create the brand, by being different, a similar position to Microsoft whose software allows users to be anything they want to be. SMS messaging is similar in that people, especially young people, create their own use of the product, such as sending messages to each other in class. As for promotions, the AI phenomenon of 'who killed Evan Chan?' (promotion for the 2001 Spielberg film *AI*) is a good example. Here the studio created Web sites and part of the trail, and the people who played the online game also created sites and added new directions to the story. The studio was fuelling, not controlling the promotion.[20]

PEOPLE CHANGE ITS SIGNALLING

At an advertising level, the original brand ads for Orange UK allowed individuals to create their own view of what the future was, rather than dictate that vision to people. This can be done negatively, as Porsche found in the 1980s when the brand became associated with yuppies. However, in the same way, people changed the signalling again and Porsche regained its place as a classic sports car. Porsche assisted this by focusing on what they were able to control: the making of the car.

Generally, this argument accommodates the view that attitudes to a brand are formed after trial, and often there are few values attached to many brands. Here people change the signalling of these messages by discounting the values brand owners try to attach to them. For some brands the alternative is simply to have a broad and active set of attributes, and buyers may use one of them in their personal creation of the brand. Usually, these brands would be low involvement.

PEOPLE ADAPT IT

Customization is a good example of people adapting the brand, and is demonstrated by the host of customization programmes on the Internet, from car companies to Nike. Interestingly, customization and brand co-creation may not always result in something the company likes. The well-travelled story of Jonah's request for Nike shoes with 'Sweatshop' sewn on the side is a good example of this. Co-creation does involve letting go of brands, and this means that brands cannot dictate or control someone's view of the brand (of course they never could). Many people may argue that Nike should have recognized this, that how its shoes are made is within the company's domain, and that its use of sweatshop labour set the preconditions for a negative response.

WE STILL NEED TO MEASURE

Any shift in control is bound to raise new questions and concerns. If we are not in control then we may need to reconsider some of our current approaches. The most obvious are marketing metrics. Critically, metrics are still important, but co-creation recognizes that we are neglecting to measure the marketing done by buyers. This requires another shift in focus, to recognize that both buyers and sellers are contributing to the value created in marketing.

This challenges everyday concepts such as brand equity, and highlights the paradox in accepting that 'brands lie between the ears of buyers', but the equity goes on the brand owner's balance sheet. Perhaps the recognition that buyers and sellers co-create brands will explain the volatility of brands as intangible assets. If buyers withdraw the value they are contributing, then the value of the intangible asset rapidly declines.

If we accept the lack of control and co-creation perspective, we should carefully assess the contribution and value created and gained by both buyer and seller. This has led to the suggestion of a value balance, which may be particularly relevant in considering issues such as the often flawed idea of cross-selling.[22] The value balance concept highlights the fact that only when both parties contribute and receive equivalent value will buyers continue to buy from the seller; if this is not the case they will buy from another.

Even with co-creation we still need to demonstrate returns on investment from the inputs of marketing. ROI and other measures that the board understands will still be required. The difference is that the greatest returns will be the result of buyers contributing or co-creating value. What companies need to remember is that this is value that is given to them by buyers, and just as they give it to the company today, they can as easily take it away tomorrow. And in today's competitive markets they may take it away for many reasons beyond product or service quality. Most likely they will take it away as an emotional response to the way the company behaves.

THANKS DAD

My old man would have struggled with the idea that marketing is just kidding itself if it believes it is in control. But I am sure he would have recognized that it fits with the massive changes in Western society, especially the rising discontent as people feel they have little control over their current situation. Perhaps he may even have reluctantly agreed that while marketing sees its side, it is often blind to the possibility that buyers also do marketing and that buyers and sellers co-create value.

The implications of this are significant, and affect all marketing activities. It demands a number of responses, including a willingness to let go of brands, to consider what we can and can't influence, and understand preconditions versus attempted control. It also suggests that we need to expand some of the current views of brand equity and where it resides.

This does not mean we have to give up control, but rather we need to recognize that marketing operates in the grey area between control and no control. In this grey area, control is passed back and forth between brand owner and buyer, and together they co-create brands. The brand owner can set the platform for this to occur and even to influence it, but it cannot ultimately control it. This is the same as the difference between leadership and dictatorship. In fact great leaders are often similar to dictators, the difference being that they know they cannot control other people, they can only set the platform for them all to create something. This means that both leaders and those around them contribute. Some brands seem to understand this and are addressing it in different ways, including customization, personalization, brands as organizational culture, leaving gaps in communication, and even letting the buyer be the brand.

No doubt many people will disagree with this view. After all, business has revelled in its competitiveness, war and sport analogies, in its hierarchies and powers of persuasion. Business leaders are supposed to be in control, they are measured by their success in creating ever larger companies. Power and control are an everyday part of business, which, in their present form will not be surrendered easily. And in many situations they should not be surrendered. But it is now time to recognize there are situations where buyers create value, and they should be encouraged to, because buyers are marketers too.

THANKS

This work is far from original as it is influenced by many people, especially Mark Earls, Anne Stephens from Yellowwood, South Africa, Denzil Myers in San Francisco, everyone who participated in our session at the US APG 2001, everyone at Nilewide and Headmint, and our many clients who are always prepared to comment, but most of all Karina, my wonderful daughter, who has taught me so much, and our fathers.

NOTES

1 Hibbard, J (1999) Buyer's market, *Red Herring* (USA) (Nov), Online.
2 Gordon, W and Valentine, V (2001) The 21st century consumer: an endlessly moving target, *Market Leader* (UK), 11, pp 50–55
3 Frank, T (2000) *One Market under God: Extreme capitalism, market populism, and the end of economic democracy,* Doubleday.
4 Cova, B (1997) Community and consumption, *European Journal of Marketing* (UK), 31 (3/4), pp 297–316.
5 Cook, R (1998) Tackling the problem of increased TV ad zapping, *Campaign* (UK), 25 Sept, p 16; Klein, N (2000) *No Logo*, Flamingo, London.

6 Customer experience fails to live up to expectations, *Customer Loyalty Today* (UK), 1 July 2000, Profound; UK public blows relationship marketing out of the water, *Customer Loyalty Today* (UK), 1 June 2000, Profound.

7 Gladwell, M (2000) *The Tipping Point*, Little Brown; Godin, S (2000) Unleash your ideavirus, *Fast Company* (USA), Aug, pp 115–35.

8 Gladwell, M (2000) *The Tipping Point*, Observation of the Account Planning Group, USA, July 2000

9 Shipside, S (2000) Infectious stuff, *Business 2.0* (UK), Aug, pp 76–80.

10 Mitchell, A (2001) *Right Side Up*, Harper Collins.

11 Kelly, R and Reed, P (2001) Brand ownership: revisiting the definition, *Admap* (UK) May, pp 42–45.

12 Phau, I and Cheen Lau, K (2001) Brand personality and consumer self-expression: single or dual carriageway? *Brand Management* (UK), **8** (6), pp 428–44.

13 Heath, R (2000) Low involvement processing: a new model of brands and advertising, *International Journal of Advertising* (UK), **19**, pp 287–98.

14 Barnard, N and Ehrenberg, A (1997) Advertising: strongly persuasive or nudging? *Journal of Advertising Research* (USA), **37** (1), pp 21–31.

15 Oliver Stone presentation to the Account Planning Group USA, July 2001, Las Vegas.

16 Hamel, G (1998) Strategy innovation and the quest for value, *Sloan Management Review* (USA), **39** (2), pp 7–14.

17 Hopkinson, G (2001) Influence in marketing channels: a sense-making investigation, *Psychology & Marketing* (USA), **18** (5), pp 423–44.

18 Ehrenberg, A (2001) Marketing: romantic or realistic? *Marketing Research* (USA), Summer, pp 40–42

19 Deal, T and Kennedy, A (1999) *The New Corporate Culture*, Texere; Collins, J and Porras, J (2000) *Built to Last*, Random House.

20 Sieberg, D (2001) Reality blurs, hype builds with Web 'AI' game, CNN.Com (USA), Online; Eng, P (2001) Search of Salla Intricate Web Games Market, ABC.Com (USA), 26 June, Online.

21 Schultz, D and Bailey, S (2000) Customer/brand loyalty in an interactive marketplace, *Journal of Advertising Research* (USA), **40** (3), pp 41–52.

Chapter 7

Brands on the brain: new scientific discoveries to support new brand thinking

Wendy Gordon

Wendy began her career in market research at JWT in South Africa before immigrating to England in 1971. Qualitative research offered a more flexible career for a working mum – and she chose to join the 'guru' of qualitative research, Bill Schlackman, who proved to be an inspirational and challenging mentor.

Wendy worked closely with Bill for 10 years before striking out with her colleague Colleen Ryan to start The Research Business International – a company which acquired a reputation for innovative research methods and empathy towards advertising and the discipline of planning. Maritz Inc acquired TRBI in 1994 and Wendy remained as company Chairman for three years, before leaping into the unknown and founding The Fourth Room, a multi-disciplinary marketing consultancy.

Wendy is a Fellow of the Market Research Society and in 1998 she was honoured by The Women's Advertising Club of London (WACL) as one of its 75th anniversary 'Women of Achievement'.

Wendy's second book, Good Thinking, *was published by Admap publications in November 1999.*

WHAT IS THIS CHAPTER ABOUT?

- Why businesses and brands are under pressure.
- Why there is a demand for 'consumer insight'.
- Looking to neuro-psychology for answers.
- Brands and brain activity – scientific facts.
- Facts demand change.

THE PRESSURE ON BUSINESSES AND BRANDS

Companies today are under huge pressure to grow profits in order to improve shareholder value and return. City analysts are ruthless when companies fail to show 12–15 per cent improvement year on year. The stridency of derision by the business media, combined with the fact that CEOs have been given substantial incentive packages linked to performance, has resulted in short-term planning. By far the easiest and quickest strategy is to strip costs from the supply side of business. This 'managing for value' corporate mantra is endemic – ruthless and systemic cost cutting and efficiency programmes which provide immediate results to the bottom line and leave management depleted, demotivated and risk averse.

After nearly a decade of incremental improvement achieved in this way, many companies no longer have any fat to trim. The organization is lean and hungry but finds itself in a strange dilemma. Firstly its competitors are lean and hungry too, so that instead of leading the pack, the company finds itself right in the middle, on equal footing with everyone else.

Secondly continual analysis of the internal operational structure and resources of the company results in a severe case of paralysis. Managers lose connection with customers – who they are, what they need, where they are going and how they see the world today. The result is wave after wave of 'creeping crap', as one UK marketing director succinctly expressed the signs of the times. Gary Hamel talks about depressing mediocrity: 'There is an ever-growing population of mediocre companies and an ever-diminishing population of truly great performers.'[1] Add the experience of mediocre brands to this quote, and we have an accurate picture of what it feels like to be an investor, manager, customer or a consumer in the UK at the beginning of the 21st century.

It is not all bad news. There are companies that are successful. These are companies that have recognized that managing the costs of a business is a necessary hygiene factor but not the secret of long-term success. They have turned their attention to ways and means to achieve growth – to increase revenue substantially while at the same time performing operationally as efficiently as possible. For these companies, brand building and business innovation is the way to achieve growth. What do these fat phrases mean? To paraphrase Humpty Dumpty, 'words mean whatever I want them to mean'.

'Brand' means packaged goods such as Radox or Persil, shops like Tesco, the Body Shop or Prêt-à-Manger, services like British Airways or Barclays Bank, utilities like ScottishPower, and entertainment or information experiences like Disney or CNN. Of course there are many other kinds of brands too – institutional brands, nation states, political parties, sports clubs, universities and individuals.

'Brand building' means growing revenue by finding new customers, creating new products/services or discovering new business opportunities.

'Innovation' means redefinition of the competitive space. Southwest Airlines redefined the way that airlines served and charged people for internal flights in the USA; Prêt-à-Manger redefined the meaning of lunchtime sandwiches in the UK. Innovation is not the slow incremental improvement that comes from line extensions, small product tweaks ('now with added…') or minute alterations in proposition or positioning. It is strategic and long-term in its vision and ambitions.

Both brand building and strategic innovation require connection or re-connection with people (that is, people who buy, interact or use the brand). The attention of the CEO or Board turns automatically to marketing and research when it comes to understanding people.

THE NEW CHALLENGE FOR MARKETING AND RESEARCH

Human beings are reassuringly similar in many ways. If someone feels inadequate or in danger of failing, he or she searches for someone else to blame rather than taking responsibility for the problem. So it is with companies. If the CEO or Board underperforms in terms of innovation or building brands, the natural culprits will be marketing and research. They in turn, look to see whom they can blame!

We don't have to look very far for evidence of this domino effect. There is a new plea for help coming from marketing and research managers within companies. It is a request for 'customer insight' – more of it, different kinds of it and the more effective use of it. But what is it? Again and again we fall into the trap of ill-defined words that seem simple to understand on the surface but hide different assumptions underneath.

'Insight' has different meanings for different people. For some it is the 'aha' moment when a particular set of information leads to a moment of understanding – clarity out of confusion. It can mean a sound plan of action; a crystal clear business or brand opportunity that becomes apparent through the identification of a consumer need. For Unilever it is a model of thinking: 'to see what everyone sees but to think what no one thinks'.

Leading account planners and qualitative researchers have always dealt in the currency of deep insight rather than deep data. Account planning was built on the concept that insight about ordinary human beings and their relationships with a brand can be translated into a relevant and distinctive (advertising) campaign. Nowadays it is becoming increasingly common for senior management to value insight too. It is seen to be an essential prerequisite for brand building or business/brand innovation.

However you define insight, it is closely aligned with imagination – they go hand in hand. Insight combined with ideas leads to exciting opportunities and possibilities. Insight is not a commodity. It cannot be found by following a formulaic process. It is not simply amassing more research, although it might be about conducting research in a different way. Insight is not something to be found like a diamond lying on a path. Insight into the way people think, feel and behave in relation to brands comes from reframing the fundamental ways in which professionals in marketing, advertising and research think about human beings, about the role of companies in their lives and about what they 'do' with brands.

HUMAN BEINGS ARE PERPLEXING

Despite the sophistication of computer technology to correlate vast amounts of data about people's lifestyles, behaviours, attitudes, demographic and psycho-graphic profiles, ordinary people remain tantalisingly unique and unpredictable. Individuals do not quite fit into segmentation stereotypes, as anyone who has ever tried to recruit people to a group using statistical cluster data will surely know. Despite the increasingly popular use of focus groups, projective techniques, observational methods and trend spotting, people are perplexingly difficult to explain, and their possible take-up of a new brand or business concept is almost impossible to predict.

Focus groups give testament to the fact that ordinary people are happy (for a fee) to play games personifying brands, creating landscapes with pens and scrap art materials, or choosing between adjectives or sentences to describe a brand. They are able, usually, to deconstruct the behaviour that you (the researcher or planner) have observed and explain why it is that they did what they did. They can look backwards and tell you all the reasons leading up to a decision, and it will seem logical and straightforward. They can even jump forward in time and construct explanations about whether a new idea will succeed or not, and sound plausible.

Then why is it that what they think and say is not what they do? Research in the early 1980s into the concept of herbal and fruit teas indicated that UK tea drinkers would never take to 'funny tea'. Yet they have. Why did research into the mobile phone market not anticipate that it was its social value rather than work usage that has driven penetration? Why does research into women's attitudes to body size consistently indicate that they want to see real women in advertisements and on the catwalk? But when plus-size women are shown, sales plummet!

The old adage that 'people don't say what they mean or mean what they say' has often been used by researchers to justify a particular methodology. In reality, no research method is foolproof when it comes to distinguishing between 'reported' intentions and opinions, and real behaviour that adapts to the changing priorities of real life.

This unsettling thought has been reinforced by the observation that ordinary people often struggle to articulate how they think and feel about brands – even very familiar ones. They find it extraordinary that we professionals are willing to talk about a brand and its competitors for hours at a stretch, and that we determinedly try to identify 'reasons why' behind brand choice.

There is an apparent paradox. What people say directly or reveal indirectly about a brand is complex and contradictory. There is all the richness of brand meaning that we glimpse in research situations, while at the same time people explain brand behaviour in terms of automatic habit, sudden impulse or inertia. It is perplexing that a particular segment of people we have identified has a low recall of the advertising for a brand despite positive pre-test results, a heavy weight of advertising, or a campaign that receives accolades in the trade press. It is odd that customers, even regular ones, show such a lack of brand loyalty and an ephemeral relationship with a service that they have used for years. It is surprising that people are so inert and resistant to change brands, even when the product or service is not very good.

It is strange that qualitative and quantitative research findings with the same objectives sometimes appear to contradict one another. Even worse, why do two different qualitative researchers reveal different aspects of a brand or even different explanations of human motivation? Is it the method or the person that causes the difference? Which one is right?

Contrast these paradoxes and ambiguities with what is talked about in meetings and on conference platforms around the world. Marketing and advertising experts talk authoritatively about brand decision-making models. Eminent researchers and thinkers present intelligent and rigorous diagrams at conferences about the structure and nature of brands – pyramids, diamonds, concentric circles and atomic models. There is a vast literature on brand loyalty, consumer–brand relationships, and how advertising works and how it can be measured. In case-study presentations, quantitative measurement is used to support major business decisions; qualitative interpretations are used to provide colour and texture.

There is marketing theory in abundance. There is also a weight of evidence that suggests that many of the fundamental concepts of traditional marketing are no longer appropriate. Existing models of thinking based on the psychology of the individual and of the social group have not succeeded in cracking these conundrums. So it is important to look elsewhere – to new fields of science.

NEURO-PSYCHOLOGY – A NEW PLACE TO SEARCH

It is not widely known that Freud was a neuroscientist who became frustrated that his chosen field of work did not help him answer some pretty fundamental questions. It was simply not possible to understand the nature of personality, internal perceptions, fantasies, motivations and the complexity of human mental life by studying the brain as an organ. For this reason he separated himself from brain science and began to develop theories of human mental life based on psychological observations and intensive involvement with his patients' views of the world – perception, beliefs, dreams, motivations, drives and actions.

The situation has now changed. Scanning technology and cognitive brain research experiments have now enabled us to understand how the brain works as never before. Although still in its infancy, neuroscience is beginning to catch up with the psychologically based sciences of the mind. We can now study the brain and gain a solid understanding of its physiology and its functions and how it makes us into human beings who can remember the past, act in the present and plan for the future – sometimes all at once.

The 21st century has seen the merging of these two disciplines, neuroscience and psychology. These have formed a new and contemporary field called neuro-psychology. This discipline has already proved directly relevant to the marketing, advertising and research fraternity. Robert Heath has explored the fact of low-involvement processing adding insight into how brands and advertising work.[2,3] Other authors have drawn on an understanding of how memory works in developing approaches to advertising pre-testing.[4]

This paper draws together the thinking of three very different people from completely unconnected backgrounds – an eminent advertising and brand specialist, a neuroscientist and a psychoanalyst:

- Giep Franzen is a well-known author and consultant on advertising and brands, and has recently published a book with Margaret Bouwman called *The Mental World of Brands*.[5]
- Mark Solms, a psychoanalyst and neuropsychologist, gave a series of 10 lectures introducing non-scientists to the brain at the Anna Freud Clinic in London.[6]

- Antonio Damasio has written several books, the most recent concentrating on the most fundamental human trait – the feeling of self.[7]

New scientific facts about how the brain and memory work allow us to begin to address a number of questions that are central to an understanding of brands. How does a brand live and die in the memory? Where does the concept of a relationship with a brand fit into mental activity? What are thoughts, emotions and feelings, and do people have them about brands in any meaningful way? What are we to think about such concepts as consciousness and the unconscious in relation to brands and brand messages? Are decisions made rationally, even for major ticket items like cars and holidays? Is the way that professional marketers, advertisers and researchers talk about brands a reflection of reality or is it all a fantasy?

THE HUMAN BRAIN AND BRANDS

The brain is a complex system. The number of connections between neurones is hyper-astronomical, which means that the brain has a large storage and processing capacity.

> Let us imagine I live in a town with 30,000 inhabitants. A phone line runs from my house to all the other houses. The same goes for each of the others. 29,999 telephone lines depart from each house. That is a complex network. You could apply that to every single inhabitant on the globe. If you take 50 terrestrial globes you might approximate the complexity of the brain.
> (Wytse J. Wadman, professor of Neurobiology at the University of Amsterdam, quoted in Aan de Brugh, 1999)[5]

Neurones form circuits. Circuits form networks. Networks form systems. Systems form super-systems. Super-systems combine to form the equivalent of galaxies.

It has been estimated that each of us has about 10,000 brands stored in the brain. This is not hard to believe when you think about how many brands we meet in everyday life – in the supermarket, the high street, on holiday abroad, through television, on the Web and so on. So what? What does this mean for brands?

- It means that a brand is one tiny insignificant star in the huge galaxy of brands stored in the brain. How can it be differentiated?
- It means that marketing professionals are too brand-centric in their thinking. They wear magnified reading glasses to look outside at what is happening in the world. Their vision is blurred and inaccurate.
- It means we need to question the measures we use to determine brand strength or brand relationships.

Although there has been a 20-year dialogue about the validity of spontaneous and prompted recall measures as criteria of brand strength, new scientific experiments can help us resolve the debate. In order to move these debates on, we need to know what a brand is – in the brain. What cellular structure does it have? How is it formed? How does it change over time?

WHAT A BRAND IS IN MEMORY

A brand in memory is the totality of stored synaptic connections between neurones. It is gradually built up through the combination of many past experiences and ongoing current encounters with a brand. People touch a brand in many different ways nowadays. Each encounter – whether above or below the threshold of conscious attention – builds on the ones before.

People observe how the company behaves towards its products/service delivery, such as whether or not it improves or cuts quality and value. They notice the way it treats staff, customers and shareholders, and who it cares about most. Word of mouth stories spread between people about the way that the company behaves in its local community, its stance on environmental issues and its ethical morality. Integrity – or lack of it – leaks through the detail of communication, irrespective of whether this is managed and paid for (like advertising, sponsorship, packaging, PR, design and so on) or unmanaged and accidental (like litter, abandoned supermarket trolleys or battered carrier bags). People experience a variety of shades of service, and know whether a particular encounter comes from the heart or has been learned by rote.

All of these experiences and brand encounters merge together to form an image of the brand that is stored somewhere in the brain. However there are different kinds of brain activity going on in different systems of the brain. It is as if we have different filing cabinets filled with different kinds of information about a brand. These are:

- Sensory perceptions – what it looks like, how it feels, smells, tastes and sounds.
- Abstract meanings – what its purpose is, what it means and how it is interpreted.
- Somatic markers – how it is coded in terms of feelings.
- Learned attitudes – what has been taught or learnt about it.
- Behavioural tendencies – what actions it provokes.

For example, each time we see a brand (a pack, logo, can or whatever), the visual stimuli are broken up and stored on both sides of the brain in different systems which have different triggers. For example there are 75 different visual modules – colour, intensity, shape, spatial dimensions, size, and so on – and each is responsible for a tiny element of the whole 'look' of the brand in the mind. The same is true of the other sensory inputs – auditory, kinaesthetic, olfactory and gustatory.

So what? A brand in the brain is nothing more than a web of connecting neurones that 'fire' together in different patterns. It is easy to forget that a brand is not an onion, a pyramid or a diagram on a page. A brand is not a Xerox, a video or a print reproduction that is 'branded' (burnt) on to one part of the brain. It is not a thing. Neither has it a fixed meaning that is 'owned' by a company or an organization. A brand is a metaphor for a complex pattern of associations that exists in the heads of individuals (customers, consumers, users, suppliers, city analysts, employees and so on).

There are five different filing cabinets of brand associations – five different kinds of brand image. We rely too heavily on learnt attitudes and behavioural tendencies. Because the others are harder to open we ignore them – the sensory and emotional image files in particular. Abstract meanings like 'convenience', 'good value' or 'luxurious' are like land-mines that easily and unexpectedly explode. Fat concepts mean different things to different people. If we assume they mean the same as the definition we carry around in our own heads, we reinforce the distance between brands and people.

PROCESSING INFORMATION ABOUT BRANDS

There is a saying in brain science: 'neurones that fire together are wired together'. The more frequently an association between things is repeated, the more likely it is that the dendrite connections between the neurones strengthen. In other words, physiological changes take place that increase the likelihood of certain patterns occurring in response to a stimulus. The converse is true too.

There is a difference between active processing of information – something that we do with full attention, holding ideas in mind and manipulating them and shallow processing of information – something that happens automatically, semi-consciously or even unconsciously. Robert Heath is a proponent of the view that most brands and advertising are processed at the shallow level: 'The Low Involvement Processing Model operates through the repeated processing of elements and concepts at low attention levels, leading to the gradual establishment of 'meaningful' association with the brand.'[8] So the contacts between person and brand are continuously and steadily building the brand memory.

MEMORY IS DYNAMIC

The total super-system is in continuous development. Neurones grow new attachments, and connections between neurones either increase in strength or weaken and fade away. It is not widely known that the brain is plastic, and its connective structure changes through experience. This is why the brain can store and process information in the way a computer is unlikely to be able to do.

This means that an item stored in memory is constantly being reorganized and recoded. Memories change depending on the nature of the stimulus for recall and the context in which the memory is being stimulated. The way we retrieve memory depends on the cue given. For example, recognition is a more powerful retriever than recall. Words, images, symbols, concepts and actions all access different parts of the brand in memory.

So what? The dynamic nature of brand memory has major implications for the disciplines of research and marketing. What people retrieve is only as good as the search engine used. Search engines are good or bad depending on who is using them. So it is with brands. What someone brings to mind depends on who they are, where they are, why the brand is being prompted, what aspects of it are relevant at that moment, and so on. What people remember and describe in a focus group environment is different from what they might recollect when interviewed at home, or what might come to mind in the context of experiencing the brand.

And to make matters more complicated, a brand means different things in different contexts. Take Coca-Cola, for instance. When I drink a Coke in a pub in the evening, I choose it because it is an acceptable adult drink-and-drive soft drink. If I choose to drink it at a summer barbecue it is because it is a refreshing drink that I strongly associate with summer. If I order it at The Ivy (or any other very sophisticated restaurant) I am probably being provocative and making a statement in front of the people I am with about my identity. Brands do not have fixed meanings. Brand associations change depending on context.

There are three points worth making strongly:

- *Cells that fire together are wired together.* Brand associations are strengthened over time through repetition (and weaken over time if not repeated). This does not need conscious attention. It can happen below the radar. We are like elephants – we never ever forget. Certain associations are indelible. Think of the Dulux dog or the Andrex puppy!
- *We encounter brands in a myriad of ways over time.* Each encounter with a brand is a stimulus that is stored in the brain and adds to the associative network that already exists. Two people can never experience an identical set of encounters with a brand, and therefore their brand engrams will be different.
- *Marketing people tend to think only of managed communications,* like advertising and other paid-for messages, to create and maintain brand meaning. Other encounters with a brand are even more important in creating brand meaning, such as the people who represent the brand (employees or other brand users), the place the brand is bought or consumed (distribution network and consumption environments) and the product/service itself (range, packaging, service attributes and so on).

THOUGHTS, EMOTIONS AND FEELINGS – EMOTIONS WIN

One of the most significant facts in neuro-science is that thoughts are never separate from emotions and emotions never separate from thoughts. Brands are coded in both cognitive AND emotional patterns in the brain and are inextricably linked.

'Emotions constitute an integrated element of the seemingly most rational decision-making. Whenever thinking conflicts with emotions, emotions win'.[5] It is now believed that emotional coding explains 'selective perception': why we notice some brands and not others. Emotions are bodily responses that go on invisibly and are detected in three ways:

- non verbal postures/expressions;
- physiological changes – fast breathing, sweating;
- sensations – that we call feelings.

Sensations and feelings indicate the presence of a deeper underlying emotion. So what? Asking people to talk about feelings is a cognitive exercise. Encouraging people to re-experience a brand in memory (by accessing the five categories of brand associations) provides a completely different set of information.

Many professionals still talk in terms of 'right and left brain' as if these were independent operating systems. They are not. They are so inter-linked that if the two hemispheres are separated through a stroke or major injury, an individual is unable to make any decisions at all. He or she can walk, read, talk, eat and sleep, but cannot function in the world as an effective adult human being. Similarly, many creative briefs separate 'reason why' from 'emotional benefit'. This may be a useful analytical exercise, but it is not the way that human beings absorb and store information.

THE IMPLICATIONS FOR RESEARCH

If neuro-science is giving us new information about what a brand is (in terms of how the brain works) then the research approaches that we are using to give us consumer insight must change. A new model of thinking about research is slowly emerging, particularly at the leading edge of qualitative practice. There is recognition that different disciplines and different kinds of enquiry lead to insight and understanding that is not possible using only one single research method.

The use of multiple strands of discovery and enquiry is called the 'bricolage' approach to research, and is widely accepted in academic qualitative practice. 'Bricolage' means 'a pieced-together set of practices' that lead to a more robust understanding of the whole. It is a pragmatic solution to illuminate possible answers to a complicated question.

Contrast this with the current approach that tries to find a single answer to a complicated question. The focus group is a symptom. So is the U&A. Simple answers are quick, useful, we can cope with them. However, when we know that brands within our memories can be accessed in different ways and the access route will lead to different associations and understandings about the brand, we have to accept that there is likely to be more than one answer. Bricolage is the perfect approach to use if the brand team is seriously interested in understanding the elements of the brand engram.[9]

Today there is a large menu of methods that make up the toolkit of a bricoleur researcher. Direct interviews with people or group discussions with many are only two of the options. Observation of behaviour in brand contexts, ethnography, NLP (neuro-linguistic programming, a model of thinking that helps to reveal the sensory representation (construction) of a brand and to explain non-verbal feelings about it), semiotics, discourse analysis, trend analysis and cultural Braille-reading all provide rich and varied perspectives on the subject of study namely how human beings create brand meaning. This incomplete list illustrates that there are many ways to reveal insights about human beings as individuals, as group animals and as cultural beings. As with all tools, there are those who learn to use them properly and those who prefer to use a hammer for every single DIY task!

Marketing professionals must take responsibility for both understanding and supporting bricolage – not only practitioner researchers. Marketing professionals hold the budgets. It is no longer justifiable (scientifically) to believe that a single research method or even a single 'guru' researcher is able 'to get under the skin of the consumer'.

New qualitative methods are particularly suited to revealing a brand (as a neuro-scientific fact). They can look at the brand landscape now and also from the past. They are multi-dimensional. They consider a network of possibilities. They are not looking for a single answer, although they may look for a unified view of responses. They recognize the importance of our past, the importance of the history in our memories and the history of our brands. They also calibrate the brand against the future – the changes that create new meaning for the brand against a dynamic world.

This means that people who use and apply research insight to business problems should think in terms of possibilities. In turn, research practitioners should have the confidence, based on scientific fact, to say they do not know all the answers, but here are a few. This leads to cross-disciplinary and shared responsibility about the 'so what's', and it leads to team workshops to apply the insights about human beings to real marketing and advertising implementation tasks. Finally and most importantly it leads to a change of mind-set – confidence in the power of imagination and intuition to create new solutions from genuine insights, rather than the analysis paralysis that stems from thinking in terms of 'data' and 'findings'.

Research is a scientific discipline, but the answers for the brand are a creative act. This book and chapter makes it clear that there is a new marketing and advertising agenda. Those of us who work with brands and who are driven by genuine curiosity live in exciting times. It is possible to connect with real human beings in real life. When we do this we have a genuine opportunity to discover powerful insights that can help businesses and brands become more relevant and meaningful to ordinary human beings like ourselves.

THE IMPLICATIONS FOR MARKETING

Four key thoughts emerge from this new understanding of the brain, and they are critical to the development of effective marketing and communication strategies.

- The history of the brand is hard-wired into the brain; we ignore this at our peril. Instead we should recognize it and build on it. We need to resist the best efforts of every new young brand manager to change the world of the brand without understanding how that world was built and which parts are essential to retain. He or she may not know, but people do, which is why every consumer can remember selling lines from decades ago ('a million housewives every day', and so on).

● There are different triggers to access brand memories. These are the search engines of the brain, and depending on the search engine the memory will have a slightly different meaning. Use the Esso Tiger as a trigger and you may get power and performance as immediate associations with the brand; use the *Exxon Valdez* and you may find that pollution and the misbehaviour of petrol companies is the strongest association. We should not discard brand triggers just because the marketing team believes that they have become tired; we should evolve them and use them. Think about how the Woolwich Building Society has evolved the long established 'I am with the Woolwich' thought.

● The emotional underpinning of a brand in memory is more important in understanding decision making than are rational associations. It is likely that the somatic marker that anchors the brand will differentiate it from its competitors, not the straight product claim. Is Kit Kat right to produce a better, easier to use wrapper (rationally) that takes away the power of (emotional) anticipation when running the fingernail down the foil paper? Perhaps we should also resist the desire to explain our product arguments rationally and tediously; much of the most powerful advertising is non-verbal and relies on an emotional, intuitive response. Think of Guinness or *The Economist*.

● Linear models of thinking about how consumers can be segmented, targeted and persuaded to buy brands are incompatible with scientific fact. The brand-centric control model is anachronistic. The way we think needs to be more holistic. Yes, the brand is responsible for sending out cues. But ordinary people are responsible for creating meaning, choosing whether or not to engage with the brand. Integrated brand communication (including the less obvious ones associated with distribution, employees, journalists, city analysts, word of mouth and other brand touch points) is a necessity, not a choice.

SUMMARY

So to summarize, how does neuro-psychology help us to rethink the consumer? Here are five headings that highlight the new learning from neuro-psychology and, hopefully, act as triggers for you to retrieve your memories of this chapter:

- Brand as a metaphor of complex associations.
- Hard wiring of brands in the memory.
- Brand triggers as search engine.
- Somatic markers to access the emotions.
- Because emotions win.

There is no absolute truth 'out there'! This is uncomfortable. If there is no absolute truth then it means that there are a number of possibilities. If we begin to work with potential scenarios or possibilities and test our thinking against them, we can make more informed decisions about the way in which people connect with brands and businesses in the real world. The real facts about brains and brands form a stronger platform for rethinking the consumer than the artificial and myopic world of marketing, advertising and research theory.

ACKNOWLEDGEMENTS

I would like to acknowledge a number of people who have helped me give birth to the thinking that is summarized in this chapter. Sally Ford-Hutchinson struggled with me to move brain science from 'interesting' to 'implications'. Much of this chapter has been adapted from the paper we wrote together and presented in October 2001.[10] Without her help I would still be mired in dendrite connections. Others helped me too by asking the 'so what?' question. This helped me to see the wood for the trees and to separate brain facts from marketing relevance. In particular I would like to thank Judy Lannon, Martin Lee, Chris Meredith and Juliet Warkinton.

NOTES

1 Hamel, G (2000) *Leading the Revolution*, Harvard Business School Press.
2 Heath, R (2000) Low involvement processing: a new model of brands and advertising, *International Journal of Advertising*, **19**
3 Heath, R (2000) 15th Annual Monitoring Advertising Performance Conference, London.

4   Branthwaite, A (2001) Direct-to-consumer advertising for ethical pharmaceuticals, *Admap*, 414.
5   Franzen, G and Bouwman, M (2001) *The Mental World of Brands: Mind, memory and brand success*, NTC Publications.
6   Solms, M (2000) *The Beginners Guide to the Brain* (video set), Anna Freud Centre, 21 Maresfield Gardens, London NW3 5SP.
7   Damasio, A (2000) *The Feeling of What Happens: Body and emotion in the making of consciousness*, Harvest.
8   Heath, R (2001) *The Hidden Power of Advertising*, Admap Publications.
9   Gordon, W (1999) *Goodthinking: A guide to qualitative research*, Admap Publications.
10 Gordon, W and Ford-Hutchinson, S (2002) *Brains and Brands: Re-thinking the consumer*, *Admap*, 424.

FURTHER READING

Damasio, A (1995) *Descartes Error: Emotion, reason and the human brain*, Avon
Franzen, G (1999) *Brands & Advertising: How advertising effectiveness influences brand equity*, Admap Publications
Gordon, W (1994) Taking brand repertoires seriously, *Journal of Brand Management*, 2 (1), pp 25–30
Gordon, W (2001) *The Darkroom of the Mind*, AQR Conference, Paris
Pinker, S (1999) *How the Mind Works*, Penguin
Valentine, V (1995) *Opening Up the Black Box*, Esomar Qualitative Seminar, Amsterdam
Valentine, V and Evans, M (1993) *The Dark Side of the Onion*, MRS Conference, Brighton

Chapter 8

Creative thinking with discipline: practical research applications from brand building theory

Mike Hall

In 1990 Mike Hall realized that although everyone agreed that advertising works in different ways, nobody had ever defined what they were. Driven to this day by an urge for original thinking, he therefore wrote what is now known as the Framework model of how advertising and brand relationships work. He wanted to provide an all-encompassing theoretical framework that would have

helped in his own 10-year career in account planning, which culminated as Planning Director of Leagas Delaney in the late 1980s.

Having started working life in research, he set up Hall & Partners as a specialist brand and advertising research agency in 1992, applying the thinking he had just developed. The agency now has offices in New York, Los Angeles and Chicago as well as London. Mike is Group Chairman and describes his role as 'creative director' of Hall & Partners.

The purpose of all marketing and advertising activity is building brand relationships. Since the currency of advertising is ideas, we make our contribution by developing ideas that will affect the fortunes of brands. There are two ways a planner can do this:

- by developing an original and powerful thought through creative inspiration, imagination or intellect, and sending the brand down that route regardless of where the brand is coming from or going to, with the conviction that the effects will in any event be positive;
- by following a discipline of thinking, using knowledge gained from research, to explore all potential avenues and identify that with the greatest potential to trigger the creative imagination about what might get the brand there in the most powerful way.

What this chapter addresses is Route 2. It may be felt that there is nothing wrong with Route 1; indeed it may to many planners have a stronger pull as using the very creativity which attracted them to the advertising business in the first place. It may also give you the satisfaction of 'owning' the idea. But I would argue that it is weaker, because it is creative thinking without discipline.

Good planning is not a random act of do-it-yourself brand building, where you might hit either the nail or your thumb equally firmly. Good planners are maximizers. What they want is not a good idea for the brand (and certainly not the first good idea they think of) but the best idea. And this means exploring all possible ideas. Which requires a discipline. It's harder work, because it's more rigorous. Route 1 planning is weaker because ultimately it's based on lazier thinking. It may be good but you don't really know how much better it would have been, and if you opted out of exploring that then you're being negligent of your brand-building responsibilities.

The discipline we need is a discipline research can partly provide. So does this mean that we can pick any research discipline? Follow the client's preferred research supplier because they know more about the arcane and frankly uninteresting process of research than you as a creative planner do? No, again not good enough. If planners are searching for knowledge, it is part of their role and responsibility to distinguish the best, or at least better, ways of getting that knowledge. It has often been said that research tends to focus on what it's good at measuring (say, spontaneous brand awareness or advertising recall) rather than on what advertisers and agencies really want to know (like, how much stronger the brand relationship has grown amongst our target of less committed users?). That's because there's a lot of lazy research thinking out there too. Following the orthodox research route isn't a recipe for doing the best for the brand either. As George Bernard Shaw said (and we had painted on an office wall): 'Orthodoxy is the grave of intelligence.'

Perhaps planners don't want to talk about research because they regard it as rather boring. They're right, it's not very interesting in itself (though it often delivers the same sort of satisfaction as completing the cryptic crossword puzzle). But the thinking behind it isn't boring. In fact it's incredibly exciting. Because it's the discipline that enables you to work out what kind of idea is going to build the brand.

So where to begin? Fortunately, this is easy because we should always start in the same place (and go back to the same place). With the state of the brand relationship. One of the reasons that research occasionally falls completely out of synch with marketing and advertising is that it fails to reflect the assumptions about the subject that it is measuring. Thus while advertisers were talking of building brand relationships, research never considered what a brand relationship was, let alone attempted to measure it.

So when I developed the Framework model, I had to find a concept to measure the brand relationship. I called it 'brand commitment', because commitment seems to describe any of the types of relationship people have. You are more or less committed to your partner, your job, a religion or a political party – and to brands.

The other concept it is useful to use is segmentation, both because everyone can understand it (useful enough in this complex area) and because it starts everyone thinking about that essential strategic planning task, targeting. The start point of any strategic planning for any brand is therefore a segmentation of commitment. All brands can be classified as is shown in Figure 8.1.

Depending on the number of people in each segment, their relative stability or volatility, and what it is that's driving or missing from that relationship with the brand, we can work out what the best brand building strategy is. As the late great Charles Channon once wrote, the best strategies are written by the people with the best understanding of the

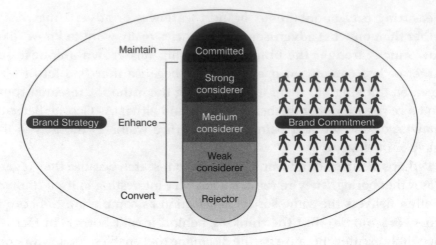

Figure 8.1 Segmentation of brand commitment

marketplace. Yet by thinking it through in this disciplined way, using research to inform that thinking, the first step is relatively straightforward.

IDENTIFYING THE BEST BRAND BUILDING STRATEGY THROUGH SEGMENTATION

Maintenance strategy

If you have a large number of committed brand users, you may decide that the strategy with the most potential for the brand is to keep the committed committed. This is essentially a maintenance strategy. Maintenance strategies often have limited appeal: if individuals already prefer you in the majority of instances to your competitor and use you as much as is appropriate in their lives, where's the potential for growth, which is needed for a return on whatever marketing and advertising investment is required?

Well, clearly we'd need to know how much our stronghold needed defending, and often the nature of the relationship and the limited returns will dictate a different type of communication strategy. British Airways has a large number of committed users, for example. During the healthy trading environment of the 1990s the strategy was one of regular, low-profile, personal communication through the Executive Club

Scheme, two for one offers and mailings. Such strategies are about justifying a premium when the market is suffering pressures of commoditization, or just protecting yourself against possible downturns. The whole concept of loyalty reward also relates to this particular strategy.

Another set of circumstances when a maintenance strategy is appropriate is when you discover that you have the opportunity for market growth. With people increasing their disposable income simultaneously with their leisure time, there may be the opportunity to get them to do even more of something they previously felt they did as much as they possibly could. (Foreign travel remains a good example, but alcohol and eating out, clothing and home entertainment all have similar opportunities occasionally.) And you might reasonably conclude that the people who might be disposed to use you more, or for something new, are those people firmly predisposed towards you to begin with.

A third occasion would be in less favourable trading circumstances, when keeping the committed committed can be more of a commercial necessity. Often this occurs with the onset of new competition. Take banking, or personal financial services as it is nowadays more cumbersomely called. Financial services deregulation in the UK allowed building societies, banks and insurance companies to offer services in competing territories previously barred to them. In the frantic period of expansion and diversification that followed, many brands forgot their existing committed users. While a building society was busy winning customers for its new current account, it forgot that existing customers using it exclusively for a mortgage were being wooed by the bank that was also now able to provide home loans. Haemorrhaging your committed users is never a good state for your brand equity, and in such a case a maintenance strategy is more than merely sensible. Getting people to re-pledge their brand vows becomes an essential objective.

Conversion strategy

At the other end of the scale are rejectors. Clearly these are people who would not consider your brand and whose preference lies (possibly strongly) elsewhere. But it is important to remember there are two types of rejector, because the strategy you pursue is often very different for the one and the other.

The first type of rejectors are individuals who know a brand, finds something about it they don't like or that doesn't work for them, and rule it out of further consideration. I am, for example, a rejector of Virgin: I dislike the attitude of the brand, which I find sly, superficial and self-regarding in all it does. I always buy my CDs in HMV, fly BA to our offices in New York, Los Angeles and Chicago and drink a 'real brand' like Coke or Pepsi.

If you were to decide that current rejectors represented the greatest potential for future growth, you would be following a conversion strategy. Once again it is seldom the main plank of an overall brand strategy, for the simple reason that it's easier to build on a positive platform than have to redress a negative balance before you can move forward. (On the whole, Virgin wouldn't waste their time and money on me.) But there are occasions when it's worth exploring in a lot more detail.

Dominant brands can often find it worthwhile. Because consumers are active brand choosers, they like to have a choice, and when they feel they haven't really got one, some people move against the dominant brand, almost on principle. Many denationalized brands had to struggle to be as strong in a competitive environment, so for a brand like BT converting rejectors offered huge potential.

This is not only because of the extra income potential converted rejectors offer, but also due to their potential to damage the brand if their rejection is not curtailed. Take the case of IBM, which once proudly – some may say arrogantly – ran an ad comprising simply a headline 'Nobody ever got fired for choosing IBM'. Not a great ad, but no problem decoding the brand strategy. Yet it produced the riposte from a rival 'And nobody got promoted either', and within a matter of a couple of years the under-lying resentment about not having a choice turned to outright rejection when Big Blue was outflanked in the PC sector. Only a strategy that showed a human face to the brand converted the rejectors and gave permission for those who felt favourably disposed to the brand to dare express their preference publicly again.

On other occasions one particular competitor can change the rules of the market and so outflank the existing leader that people switch allegiance and the new Number two brand must convert its sudden influx of rejectors. There are some classic recent cases in UK retailing: Sainsbury's was toppled as supermarket brand leader by Tesco, when the latter changed the market rules from price and value versus quality and range to being all about service (astonishingly, a radical new concept to UK retailing and the long suffering and sceptical British consumer!) While some committed users of Sainsbury's slipped into treating the store merely as a repertoire brand, which was bad enough, others abandoned their favourite completely and with barely a backward glance. What yesterday was perceived as confident today smacked of complacency. So converting the rejector became for Sainsbury's less a strategy than a mission.

Of a different type is a brand like Adidas, candidate at the start of the 1990s for a starring role in a 'Where are they now?' feature of famous brands of the 1970s. I well remember my first pair of Adidas rugby boots in 1969: customer satisfaction was not a concept around at the time but it is a feebly inadequate means of expressing the rapturous pride with which I embraced that brand. Fifteen years later my commitment to the brand remained undimmed. But this was its undoing: sadly for the brand (though not for me) I had grown middle aged, and the brand had grown middle aged with me, instead of recruiting new acolytes and advocates. The average 14 year old dismissed Adidas as 'what my dad wears'. Meanwhile Nike appeared, changed the rules from being about performance to about cool, and Adidas was off the teenage radar screen. Converting rejectors was a necessity rather than an attractive option.

But there is another type of rejector altogether, and in this instance a conversion strategy is by definition the only option. For a new brand launch there are many who say 'I wouldn't consider it because I don't know it (or don't know of it at all)'. If you were signing up to your first mobile phone in the 1990s, a little unsure of this new technology thing that might end up costing you a lot of money and make you look a bit brash and nerdy in public, and there really wasn't much to choose between the established players of Vodafone and Cellnet, why bother with these people you've never heard of called Orange?

Although it's a position faced by all new brands, many can often leverage some kind of brand connection (the Ka brand was new, but the Ford umbrella brand was not), but sometimes you can't, and a degree of market commoditization (that is, price as the major brand differentiator) merely exacerbates the situation. This was what faced Toshiba when it launched in the UK, and a bit of unhealthy British xenophobia made it no easier for the umpteenth Japanese brand to stake its market claim. And of course it was what lay behind the (not very good) strategic thinking for many of the dot.coms in the 2000/2001 feeding frenzy, and explains why so many failed so disastrously, to the great discredit of account planning in most instances.

Enhancement strategy

For most people in relation to most brands most of the time, what we are faced with is an enhancement strategy: a brand exists, people know it exists and are quite prepared to consider using it; on the other hand so do a good handful of others, and nowadays none of them is exactly bad at doing what it's supposed to do – it's just that any given person on the whole likes one or two other brands a bit more. The brand strategy (and the role of advertising) is to enhance its status in the repertoire, so that it is the generally preferred, or one of the favoured, brands, or one that you'd always put on a notional shortlist before making a final choice. It's true for mass brands and niche brands, for steady traditional brands and aggressive challenger brands; for consumer durable brands like Ford and Audi; for FMCG brands, retail brands, telecomms brands and so on.

So how you plan to build the brand relationship clearly depends on the state of the relationship to begin with. (It's amazing how few clients and planners actually know this before they embark upon a strategic review or development exercise.) And with the amount of information and creative research thinking available, there's really no excuse for not establishing this pretty accurately.

USING RESEARCH TO INFORM YOUR JUDGEMENT

How? Well, it should be clear that you need to start with how many are in each segment, so you need quantitative research. You can use behavioural data only (heavy/medium/light/non users from BMRB's Target Group Index, for example), but the advantage of measuring brand commitment is that it contains an attitudinal component too: a brand relationship can best be defined in terms of attitude to use.

This requires a tailor-made study. It doesn't matter whether it comes from your tracking study or a specially commissioned positioning/segmentation/attitude and usage/brand equity study – a brand commitment question should be in all of them, because like Rome it's where all roads lead to.

This is where you should beware the orthodox or reflex response. Some research agencies insist that you should always use exactly the same consideration question for all brands in all markets, using a standard five-point scale when the top point always reads something like, 'It's the only brand I'd ever consider buying', or even worse, a crass 'intention to purchase' question, 'I'd definitely intend to buy this brand next time'. Now it's possible that this might work for washing powder, or coffee granules, where people might want to identify the one brand they feel delivers best for them and stick with it. But consider how silly it is for beer, chocolate, cereals or shampoo. In repertoire markets the aim is to have a high status in the repertoire, not to expect a degree of preference that leads to rejection of all other contenders. Then try it for size with television channels, Yellow Pages or government brands like Energy Efficiency or the Army. Lazy thinking leads to lousy thinking.

It is obvious that to measure brand commitment you need a scale that reflects the actual consideration process that takes place in that market. It needs to reflect the way consumers talk about the market, not be written in research-speak. The whole concept of 'purchase intention' reflects outdated assumptions about highly mechanistic consumer behaviour. It simply doesn't reflect the way consumer–brand relationships work.

Getting the question right is an art (one of those satisfying crossword-solving moments) where you should use the skills of well-trained researchers. But planners can help by formulating and articulating their assumptions about desired responses. It's your first draft of your working hypothesis.

DEVELOPING A HYPOTHESIS GIVES YOU A DISCIPLINE

In a recent book I have co-written for the IPA, we identified the basic principles of what makes good advertising, called shared beliefs.[1] (They are not just personal opinion, but come from talking to the great thinkers and doers of our industry.) Those relating to developing a good strategy can provide helpful guidelines here, and the very first shared belief in the book states simply 'Start with an end in mind'.

The set of shared beliefs is not just a collection of headlines, but rather it examines why each principle holds true and explains its implication for doing better advertising. And in explaining why it is a good principle to 'start with an end in mind' we wrote: 'Advertising is not a mechanistic process, but a voyage of discovery. You don't know for sure where you are going until you get there. But you do need to start with a plan. Because even the first step you take, takes you in a certain direction. The start point is to develop a working hypothesis.'[2]

The reason that this is so important is that it leads to your identifying your assumptions about what type of response to the brand you need to strengthen the relationship, and thus what type of advertising communication you need in order to stimulate that response. These assumptions are your 'model' of how advertising will work to build the brand. And any research needs to reflect these assumptions if it is to give the most helpful guidance for strategic development – or, in other words, for refining that working hypothesis.

This is the value of the Framework model of the different ways of building brand relationships through advertising. This philosophy, which I developed in 1991, is now universally used, so any reader unfamiliar with the theory is referred elsewhere. It identified four different 'models', which are four different types of assumption or hypothesis (see Figure 8.2). In summary they are:

- Sales response: the assumption that the best way to build the brand relationship is by stimulating short-term behavioural response to promotional offers (in effect long-term brand building being replaced by a series of short-term responses).
- Persuasion: the assumption that what will strengthen the brand relationship most is a belief in the functional superiority of your brand, stimulated by a demonstration or communication of the 'reason why' it performs better.
- Involvement: the assumption that the brand relationship will be built most strongly neither by believing in nor identifying with the brand, but simply responding to its sense of momentum or leadership.
- Salience: the assumption that we can force a reappraisal of the brand relationship by creating a sense of leading the way in the market by advertising that stands out as very different.

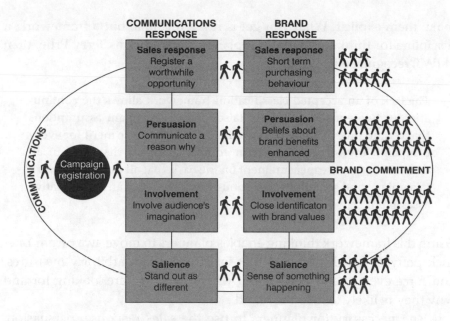

Figure 8.2 The Framework model

The models are a practical help in following another shared belief about what makes good advertising, relating to strategy: 'Identify a target response not just a target audience'. It is not sufficient to work out that it is those with a weak-to-middling relationship with the brand whom you wish to target: 'The start to any effective strategy is to work out what kind of response you want from these people.... Then give them a stimulus they will want to respond to.' And this is where the models really help, because they provide the rigour to ensure that we explore all of the possible drivers before deciding what is likely to trigger the stronger commitment we desire.

EVERYONE USES MODELS IMPLICITLY

In some quarters recently there has been a certain amount of resistance to the concept of models, with certain researchers claiming that 'planners don't use models'. This is unhelpful nonsense. Models aren't 'boxes' that we're trying to force creative thinking into. They're actually *your* models. I identified them by asking advertising people to state their assumptions. Everybody in advertising uses these models implicitly; what I did was to make them explicit. What you get is not a formula, but a framework, a discipline for thinking. Without it planners are stuck as Terry Prue, then at JWT, recognized in 1987:

> The lack of an accepted classification framework allows the continuation of two equally unhelpful falsehoods: i) Arrogant assumptions that certain intermediate measurements have intrinsic merit for every campaign investigated.... ii) An equally arrogant dismissal of all consumer response measurement on the basis that all campaigns work in a unique and somehow mysterious way that defies any quantitative assessment.[3]

Using this framework thinking enables planners to move away from 'one-trick pony' research packages that insist on certain arbitrary measures, and force everyone to think about what effects we are looking for and why they're likely to help the brand.

It isn't necessary for planners to use the sales response, persuasion, involvement and salience labels that people at Hall & Partners use, but it is necessary for you to articulate your assumptions in one form or another, for the simple reason that if you don't state your assumptions then research can't reflect them. And then it's not measuring the right things. Articulating your assumptions doesn't strike me as particularly difficult, but not doing so leads to lazy thinking. It's a rigorous process that leads you to challenge your own assumptions and others to do the same, in a way that hones them to a fine point. It's just good, honest, hard work. The joy is not just that it leads to much better research, but that as a consequence the research leads to much more focused guidance. To explain how, and how you can use the thinking, we need to look separately at the different stages in the brand-building cycle, which require different types of research study.

APPLYING DISCIPLINED THINKING TO BRAND POSITIONING RESEARCH

Let us begin with the early stages of developing a brand building strategy. Let us assume you have identified which segment might have the most potential from a tracking or segmentation study but we don't know precisely the nature of the current relationship and what might trigger a more positive response.

Because the models are a framework for thinking, not a 'pre-testing technique' or any other kind of research methodology, they can be used in different applications, including qualitative research, to explore both the current brand essence and future brand avenues. In fact when I first developed them I felt that models had more potential for qualitative research, because it is so fragmented and the emphasis is put on sympathetic or individualistic moderators rather than on rigorous thinking. Whatever initial hypothesis you begin with, using these models forces you to test all options, not just one predetermined route. In one sense I disagree with the orthodox research view that you should always test the brand (or ad, or whatever) against the objectives set for it. If the objectives are wrong, then good research should point this out and give a better alternative set too.

If, for example, you're developing a strategy and by the time you get to the research you've agreed with the client that it's about contemporizing the personality, research that 'meets the objectives' will explore current personalities and relate them to market status, product performance, consumer needs, usage, lifestyle and so on, before identifying a personality that will evoke a stronger appeal. There is no discipline to force that research into thinking about whether there is a product performance characteristic that might work more strongly, or whether a radical new perspective would create a momentum that would leapfrog competitors and take the brand to the leading edge. A framework of different brand drivers does force this – it avoids the research results becoming a self-fulfilling prophecy which (occasionally) misses the mark altogether.

As well as forcing you to evaluate all possible strategies, this way of thinking also helps the research be more precisely diagnostic. A lot of advertising and brand thinking is rather vague and woolly: 'We need to be really ground-breaking and change the rules for the market' or 'We need a much more contemporary, sympathetic personality that relates to people's emotional needs', for example. None of this means very much. It needs substance and detail, and this is how to use models – to force yourself to think 'How, exactly?'

There isn't a standard formula of questions and techniques, because in detail every brand strategy is unique. But the models, acting as a typology of assumptions, allow us to focus on the precise nature of involvement (say) that we're looking for, because there are so many different ways that people can engage with a brand. Are they getting involved through shared identification, aspiration or more superficial simple association? Is this with a personality or an attitude? What are the precise dimensions of that attitude? And what are the precise dimensions of what that attitude is not? What other things or people have that attitude? And what goes with them? And what does that say about the brand? And so on. I hope this illustrates that a discipline can be a stimulus for, not an obstacle to, creative thinking.

TURNING INSIGHTS INTO ADVERTISING IDEAS

Because this discipline forces you to explore every option, it produces a wealth of information. What is it that you're looking for at this point? Not just data, but ideas.

One of the most important shared beliefs relates to this point in strategy development: 'Find a truth and make it matter.' In the book we were careful to be very precise with words (to avoid the sort of woolly thinking I am criticizing). Originally somebody said 'Find a truth that matters', but this is where planners and research often go wrong, confusing a differentiating brand essence with a strategic idea for the brand (and its communication). Planners must do something with the truth they unearth from research, in order to stimulate the creative teams to come up with a creative idea that makes that brand truth matter.

The other shared belief that relates to strategic development that provides a helpful discipline is this: 'The best advertising has a single-minded idea.' Because people take out so many things about a brand from a piece of communication, it is tempting to put in too many things as key drivers. Only one thing drives response at any one point in time. Having got there, people proceed to make many other connections, to form that rich set of residual impressions that create a brand. Strategic research may dimensionalize and specify these impressions, but it is vital to separate them from the single-minded idea. You can only get there by hard thinking, but I would argue that the discipline of models would help.

Indeed the model you choose is part of the strategic idea, because this has two elements – the strategic focus and the strategic direction. When Bernbach chose reliability as his strategic idea for VW in the 1960s, this was only part of the solution. It provided his strategic focus (what to make the brand and its advertising about), but not the strategic direction (how best to communicate it). He could have followed product demonstration as part of his strategy or glossy dramatic showcasing, but instead he decided to involve people in values they shared with the brand. (Just look at the DDB archive of ads like 'Lemon' or 'How does the driver of the snowplough get to the snowplough?') Although he didn't use my terms, his Involvement model was part of his strategic idea, and part of its strength was its single-mindedness.

APPLYING THE THINKING FOR BETTER TRACKING STUDIES

So at the other end of the development life-cycle, when you're evaluating performance against strategy, you still need to follow the same discipline of measuring all responses, not just an arbitrary few, because people don't necessarily respond in the way it's written in the strategy. And you need to know where their responses have led them, in order to refine your current hypothesis further.

Again the brand's the thing. To cite another shared belief: 'Ultimately the aim is for people to do something.' We make the point in that book that what people do often relates to mental rather than physical behaviour – changing or reconfirming their commitment, as we saw in different strategic scenarios at the start of this chapter. And as we also saw, what drives their relationship – whether to maintain commitment, convert rejection or enhance consideration – can be a number of different types of brand response. So tracking research must measure what I term brand persuasion, brand involvement and brand salience if it is to explain brand commitment.

How you do so depends on your precise assumptions, but again there are some basic principles to act as a guide:

- At the first, summary, level of measurement, you need to use scales, because people seldom have all-or-nothing relationships with brands (these relate to outdated mechanistic concepts like 'brand loyalty' or 'brand switching').
- A brand persuasion scale is attempting to measure whether your brand (or its key competitors) has genuinely superior product performance,

and must therefore be tailored to individual markets and the key performance characteristics.

- A brand involvement scale that attempts to measure identification and qualitative techniques such as brand personification helps – but you need to ensure that it reflects whether people identify with brand personality or brand attitude, for example, and reflect this in the question.
- A brand can achieve salience through its sense of leadership, dynamic momentum or radical difference, and this should be reflected in the scale.
- Beware of over-simplification of the dynamics into 'rational', 'emotional' and 'different'. Volvo spent years making a functional argument about safety, but it was always emotional; conversely VW sought to involve people in its reliability and there was a lot about the appeal that engaged at a rational level! 'Difference' alone can easily be confused with sheer product distinctiveness – many a P&G brand was different but lacked salience in the past. Research can be complicated not because it's trying to over-intellectualize advertising and brands, but because it needs to be precise.

These questions (and proper analysis) will identify key dynamics, but for real strategic guidance you need deeper diagnostics. Which functional characteristics discriminate or act as entry thresholds? What sort of attitude or personality do people get involved with? Do they share it already or aspire to it? Is the salience of the brand driven by innovation or momentum or mere presence?

These are the brand impressions we need to cover that are related uniquely to your market. (You don't have to reinvent the wheel – there are many common factors between markets – but there is also a difference between a disciplined and a formulaic approach.) Measuring these impressions is part of the researcher's art (so at my company, for example, we developed a form of impressionistic questioning to reflect the way brand associations are held) and again it is the planner's duty to challenge the research orthodoxy about 'brand image' batteries and other default techniques.

One of my favourite challenges to planners and clients can serve as an example: 'Spontaneous (unaided) brand awareness is the most useless research measure ever invented, yet the only question included in every tracking study.' Why do I take this stance? Because it tells you nothing about the state of the relationship: just because when asked to name five car marques, you think of Ford, doesn't mean you'd consider them. What matters is the quality of awareness, which led us to invent the 'spontaneous (unaided) consideration' question. When was the last time you thought about what brand awareness actually measures? It measures brand presence, which is part of the salience of a brand – in fact many established brands with presence have high awareness but low brand momentum (like, at times, IBM, Sainsbury's and Adidas in my examples earlier). So by being very clear about what it is that we're measuring, we very quickly get to learn about useful strategic direction and what drives it.

BECAUSE THEY'RE PRINCIPLES, THEY ALWAYS APPLY

Limitations of space, and indeed your interest, mean I won't expand further here on technical implications for the design of a tracking study. Remember, you don't have to write the questions, just articulate the assumptions for your brand and its market. Especially if you've created a model you think is new and needs a new type of measurement.

The same principles apply when you're looking at ad responses as when you're measuring brand responses. (Here it's even more important to separate your strategic assumptions from your executional assumptions, and to include media as well as creative assumptions.) And the same principles apply in the development phase between identifying the brand strategy and tracking the brand and advertising status. Exploring new creative ideas in qualitative creative development research or in quantitative copy-testing uses the same conceptual measures, because you don't have a different set of assumptions – they're just at an earlier stage.

Follow a discipline like this and you'll not only end up a better planner, but more importantly you'll maximize the potential of your brand, always with a clear idea of where to go next and what to do. It's a discipline that will remain up to date because it changes to reflect how your assumptions change. The principle of reflecting assumptions is what is unchanging – it makes research tailored and flexible and focused, and treats it, like advertising, not as a mechanistic process, but a voyage of discovery.

NOTES

1   Mike Hall and Claire Bickerton (2002) *Shared Beliefs: Agency thinking about what makes good and great advertising*, IPA [Online] www.ipa.co.uk
2   Mike Hall (1998) *New Steps on the Advertising Timeline*, USAPG Conference.
3   Terry Prue (1987) Where is the 'scientific method' in the measurement of advertising effect?, *Admap*.

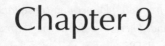

Chapter 9

Getting out of line: some techniques for creative brand thinking

Karen Hand

Having started her career in brand management in P&G, Karen's first planning challenge was trying to get any agency to believe that she could embrace creativity. After seven rounds of interviews, Still Price Lintas gave her a break as a planner on Unilever and IBM. She then moved to BBH where she worked her way up to Board Planner on accounts like Phileas Fogg, Heineken and Polaroid. With Cindy Gallop, she won the APG Grand Prix and International Gold for Creative Planning on Polaroid in 1995. She left London

in 1998 to return to Ireland and work as a freelance planner and consultant (aka Curly Enterprises). Highlights have included her work on Smirnoff brand positioning, understanding the Guinness and UDV cultures and on defining the Cirque du Soleil corporate vision and portfolio strategy, with BBH Futures and Spectrum Consultants. She is passionate about the creative potential in people, brands and cultures.

PROLOGUE

'I'll do anything except Plasticine.' This was how an MD introduced himself at a recent away day to explore the potential futures of his brands. In a brief sentence he managed to sum up the slight scepticism that many people feel about 'wacky brainstorm techniques', while demonstrating his willingness to give it a go.

His comment sparked off a number of questions. Why are we trying to be more creative in our brand thinking? What techniques and practices might we use? What factors are holding us back from using them? And how can we create cultures that encourage more differentiated brand thinking? This chapter cannot provide all of the answers but hopefully, it can help each client, agency and consultancy to ask the right questions: do we need to be more creative in our thinking, and (if yes), how are we going to create an environment to accelerate this?

THE NEED TO BE MORE CREATIVE IN OUR BRAND THINKING

The world is getting smaller. Markets and categories are converging – whether you sold groceries or mobile phones in the past, there is a high likelihood that you will be selling 'life management' in the future. Companies are buying similar quantitative data to their competitors. Qualitative research can end up repeating itself year upon year. Whereas there is always a chance that we will suddenly see the same information in a new way, there is also a nagging worry that we may not.

How do we continue to create and sustain successful brands in this climate? How do we keep our brands unique and special versus 'the rest'? How can we ensure that our brand thinking is not merely a carbon copy of our equally informed 'competitors'? Certainly we can try to be more logical than our peers and interpret the trends more speedily. However, it seems likely that we are also going to need to think differently from others if we are to find unique motivating positionings for our brands.

A DEFINITION OF CREATIVE BRAND THINKING

Creative brand thinking is 'thinking which looks at the meaning or role of a brand in a new and motivating way'. This new thinking does not have to be new to the world, just new to the brand in question. For example, Swatch were the first to look at watches as 'disposable fashion'; Apple were first to look at computers as 'home furniture'. However, the thinking should be unique and motivating for consumers, employees, and suppliers rather than simply intellectually satisfying for the brand thinkers.

As in many areas, there is a debate in the field of 'creative thinking' that looks at 'nature versus nurture'. The 'nature' camp holds that creativity is an artistic talent and you either have it or you don't. The 'nurture' camp (most famously, Edward De Bono) would hold that creativity can be learnt by anyone by using systematic 'lateral thinking' techniques. In this chapter I try to reflect both camps. I believe that some individuals will always be 'naturals' and have more flair for creative thinking. I have also worked in groups with (so-called) 'non-creative' people and watched them generate excellent ideas by using techniques.

A BRIEF LOOK AT THE BRAIN

Scientists will tell us that our brain is divided into two halves – the left side of the brain and the right side of the brain. Split-brain studies have allowed them to ascertain the characteristics of each side:

Left side	Right side
Intellect	Intuition
Convergent	Divergent
Propositional	Imaginative
Linear	Non-linear
Analytical	Holistic
Objective	Subjective

(Source: J E Bogen)

Whereas the left side of the brain concerns itself with gathering data, analysis and evaluation, the right side is far more concerned with making connections, synthesis and exploration. Both sides are important if we are to use our brains optimally. The right side helps release our intuition and imagination and the left side helps us 'post-rationalize' our findings within logical frameworks.

Ideally, the two sides work in balance and harmony (mirroring the Chinese elements, yin and yang: see below). Importantly, this is a dynamic symbol where practising thinking on one side can help you think better on the other side. For example taking a painting or music class can help you see/hear more interesting patterns when you look at data or listen to focus groups.

Yang	Yin
Masculine	Feminine
Aggressive	Yielding
Cold	Warm
Conscious	Unconscious
Left brain	Right brain
Reason	Emotion

(Source: I Ching)

However, the Western education system tends to over-emphasize the left brain (verbal and numerical reasoning) and ignores the right brain. By the time most children are 9 or 10, they have been trained out of using their right brain. This explains why many children paint happily when they are young but later they will judge themselves as 'bad at art'.

TECHNIQUES AND PRACTICES FOR CREATIVE THINKING

Don't search for Truth, simply stop having opinions.
(Source: Zen – Koan)

Edward de Bono coined the term 'lateral thinking' to describe a systematic process to help people break out of linear, left-brain thinking. He designed specific tools to help access our creative right brains and create fresh answers. Since then, various techniques have been developed to help groups and individuals access their right brains and think more creatively. At the same time people have been successful with certain practices in the workplace. These techniques and practices appear to fall broadly into the following four categories.

Scientific

De Bono's techniques are very structured and almost scientific. They appeal to rational thinking cultures because they explain why the technique works and link it to the theory of the brain. For example, his 'Po technique' takes left-brain assumptions such as 'furniture is a life time investment', then asks you to reverse them and create a right-brain world where the opposite is true, for example 'furniture changes daily', and imagine what that world would look like. From there, you can work with both your left and right brain and see the implications for your brand or your category: such as modular designs, multiple colour changes, and trade-in deals.

These structured verbal techniques are very good for encouraging people to keep their strategic options open and to use their imaginations on brand strategy before settling on a final direction. On a practical work level, people can get some of this latitude by writing a five-year strategy for their key competitor, or writing a business plan for a management buy-out.

Intuitive

Other people have come up with less verbal techniques. These vary from art therapy inspired by Rudolf Steiner (the experimental educator), where the brand thinkers are asked to describe the category/brand context using a simple painting/drawing, to Kay Scorah, co-founder of Have More Fun, getting groups to create a sculpture or a Plasticine model of 'the ideal video game experience'.

These techniques can help the group to see problems in new ways. For example the mascara category has always seen itself in terms of lashes – curling, lengthening, thickening. Through building models and collages, the client started to see the lashes as a 'tunnel' and refocus the mascara benefits away from the lashes and on to the eyes. Techniques like On Your Feet's improvisation (see Chapter 10) can also help brand development. With a company like Orange they helped translate the ethereal concept of 'brand character' into a series of concrete actions for employee behaviour.

The strength in these non-verbal techniques is that the individual or group is forced out of the left-brain world of verbal rhetoric into an attempt to express the 'holistic' brand/category situation as he/she sees it. Also useful in intuitive techniques is the chance for each team member to become aware of his or her own subjective feelings and prejudices about the brand/category, for example 'I can't wait to get my hands on one' versus 'I think they are the most pointless gadgets ever invented.'

In practical terms, we can get similar intuitive insights by 'immersing' ourselves in a brand or category. I once worked on a pitch where the clients made us study the market for six weeks before they told us anything about their new brand. Initially frustrating, we soon discovered that a given woman's cosmetic decisions are influenced by an entire 'sisterhood' (a diverse group of women ranging from her friends, colleagues and powder-room to super-models, magazines, make-up artists and Hollywood). We characterized the market as a 'web of influence', which then helped us develop more finely spun brand strategies at the next stage.

Physical

This right-brain approach to environment seeks to alter group thinking by altering how each person feels and relates to things. As Kay Scorah says, 'To really change how your mind works, you need to change how your body works.' She believes that by altering the physical space around a person, you help that person to think in a more spatial (right-brain) mode. Incorporating physical activities like juggling and yoga challenges the conventional school of away days where people are brought to a new place in new clothes but their office ('pen and paper around a table') behaviour remains unchanged.

Nevertheless, it is important to understand where these 'environmental' techniques fit in the creative thinking process. No one tool is supposed to provide answers by itself, but works with a subtle mix of factors to maximize creative potential. On a practical work level, it is also useful to move around to do your work. Your brain gets re-energized by moving to another part of the building or doing some thinking in a café or at home.

Random

As an individual, it can also be useful to harness aspects of your leisure/relaxation to help create a personal 'right-brain' environment. It is really just using your life as a continuous stream of random stimulus. So, for example, try to link the brand in question to a random movie or book or news item or coffee bar or deep massage. Use these new viewpoints to help see the problem in new ways. What (if anything) would you want from the insurance market after a massage? What would be the ideal supermarket inspired by a coffee shop?

Why not use some of the 'research' budget to search the minds of unconventional thinkers, beyond the fields of marketing and brands, at the outer edges of art, technology and science? These people don't have to be wacky or famous – they just need to have an interesting world-view. Sometimes a random person has the candour to speak the unfashionable. On an away day for an alcohol company, a faith healer was invited along. Later when the group were asking themselves 'What do young people want', she was the one person who said 'They want to be loved.'

Why not immerse ourselves in challenging environments? It might be a holiday to Bolivia, a music festival or a trip to Billingsgate fish market in the early hours of the morning. If nothing else, these right-brain forays refresh the left brain, and one is better able see situations with fresh eyes Indeed literally sleeping on it is probably the easiest way to access your right brain, especially during rapid eye movement. (Paul Valéry, the poet and philosopher, woke every morning before dawn and wrote down the first thing that came into his mind.)

The power of sleep has been harnessed in research by BBH Asia Pacific. In Asia it can be difficult to get focus groups to show their true feelings, as there is a stronger reluctance to stand out from the group. BBH initiated 'dream research' with Lisa Morgan from The Seventeen Project, where they got young people to dream and then after they woke up to draw their images of the future (see Figure 9.1). This research inspired a brand strategy for MTV Japan that was about fostering a sense of 'connectedness'

Figure 9.1 Dream research – BBH Asia Pacific

and 'community' for Japanese youth. This influenced the building location, tone of programming and type of promotions.

In practice, random groups can often develop interesting solutions in informal conversations. This is particularly likely when there is strong mutual respect and trust between the parties and 'agendas' are minimized.

THE BARRIERS TO CREATIVE THINKING

So we have a general need to think differently and a set of techniques and practices that can help us to think differently. Everything should be set for a creative brand thinking revolution. Yet despite hype about the Age of Creativity, the evidence for a step-change in brand thinking seems thin on the ground. Which then raises the question: what's stopping many brand thinkers from deliberately making these techniques and practices part of their day-to-day jobs?

Habit

Most brand thinkers believe that creative thinking is a great idea in theory, but in practice we find that we have been conditioned, throughout our education and career, to overuse our left brain. Habit kicks in each time we approach a new brand problem and we tend to dive into left-brain analysis. Of course this analysis is valuable, but it is easy for people to get bogged down in the data.

On a group level, our left brains train brand thinking teams to look at problems in standard (proven) ways. So an original strategic approach like Levis, Nike or Clark's (shoes) becomes 'let's do a Nike' (standard formula) on countless other brands. It is interesting that it is often the presence of 'obstacles' (such as a small media budget – Haagen Dazs – or terrible brand image – Skoda) that introduces a spanner into the works of smooth left-brain thinking and forces the right brain to create a more lateral and original strategy.

As David Keating, movie director and writer, says, 'It's got to the stage in Hollywood where people come up with a formulaic plot and then force-fit the characters into this story-line... really different script writing tends to happen when you start by creating interesting, unusual characters and then see what happens to the storyline when those characters interact.'

Fear

Fear can stop the adoption of lateral thinking on a general or a specific level. On a general level, some people or cultures are risk averse or conservative by nature, and even though they appreciate the idea that you need to take risks to be creative, they find it hard to take risky decisions in practice. (As an agency planner said, when interviewing a conservative brand manager for a potential move to account planning, 'It's all very well admiring brave strategies like Stella Artois ("reassuringly expensive") but would you have the guts to say "yes" to this strategy?'). These are some thoughts to help manage fear.

Multiple options

Develop frameworks that allow simultaneous exploration of high and low risk strategies. For example when BBH/Futures and Spectrum worked with Cirque du Soleil, they constructed a matrix to look at 'four futures' for the company. Using this matrix they were then able to bring to life four distinct (positive) ways that the company could develop (see Figure 9.2). They were also able to bring these four futures to life by showing how the company founders might make the front page of a different magazine for each of the four futures: for example, if they developed their product (shows) they might end up in *Variety*, if they developed their brand (multimedia) they might end up in *Le Monde* (see Figure 9.3).

As Roisin Robothan Jones, founder of Rapley, Smith and Jones, says, 'Looking at multiple strategic options is like you've got one foot on the ground while you're playing around with where to put the other foot... it feels a lot easier than jumping straight off a cliff'.

Multiple Options – Cirque Du Soleil – Four Futures

Product

Future 1: Push boundaries and make new 'live shows'	Future 2: Exploit organizational capability and help produce other people's 'live shows' eg Cats

Art ———————————————————————— Commerce

Future 3: Start pushing the boundaries in other areas – amazing films, books, clothes etc	Future 4: Milk the existing equity by making merchandising etc

Brand

Figure 9.2 Cirque du Soleil: four futures
Source – BBH Futures/Spectrum Strategy
Consultants – 1999

Figure 9.3 Four futures front pages for Cirque du Soleil

Risk-friendly cultures

Make it clear within the behaviour of the company that creativity, risk and mistakes are inevitable bedfellows. For example, there is the famous story of the IBM employee who made a mistake that cost the company $1.5

million. When he tried to resign on the back of this, his manager forced him to stay, saying, 'You are now our most expensively trained employee.'

Ownership

> We stand in our own shadows and wonder why it is dark.
> (Source: Zen – Koan)

Resistance to creative processes also arises when there are individuals who feel strongly about the existing/previous brand thinking. Quite often this is because they have had to go through some ordeal (such as a pitch process, or countless internal reviews) to arrive at that expression of the brand essence or strategy. This investment of personal energy can make them highly defensive about the *status quo*, and fearful that creative explorations may cost them their sense of certainty and control. Getting them to think in imaginary ordeal situations can be the solution to getting them to think again. For example, let's imagine that we were pitching for the business. Imagine our biggest competitor stole a march on us. How would we think then?

At times, a brand team or agency team creates its own group thinking culture, where assumptions are taken for granted and can no longer be seen by insiders. These assumptions (such as that fashion brands must show people) become 'truths' which appear strange to the outsider or new joiner.

> A fish only discovers its need for water when it is taken out of it. Our own culture is like water to a fish. It sustains us. We live and breathe through it.
> (Fons Trompenaars, Charles Hampden-Turner)

If the group culture is very entrenched, it can quite often be hostile to fresh thinking and the fresh thinker (see Figure 9.4). It is incredibly important for lateral thinking that we do not let our group thinking culture suffocate us. Some ways to minimize this include:

- Jerry Maguire manifestos – deliberately asking new joiners to propose a new brand strategy on the basis of their impressions and observations as a non-contaminated 'outsider'.

Figure 9.4 Fresh thinking

- 'Trash the strategy' away days. Invite the team and a random group of outsiders and come up with all of the reasons why the brand thinking is 'wrong'. The explicit purpose of the day can help 'insiders' to see the brand with fresh eyes.
- Internal pitches – get another group of people in the company to put together their thoughts on your brand as if they were planning to take it over. Again it is important here that the original team 'owns' the process, so that the new team's views are seen as fresh insights rather than personal attacks.
- Re-hiring yourself – this is what Adam Morgan, founder of Eat The Big Fish, called 'doing a Grove', based on the example of the Intel CEO who fired himself on a Monday and then re-hired himself on the Tuesday and looked at the company's situation with fresh eyes.

Discomfort

Moving from left-brain to right-brain mode is like switching gear, so there is likely to be an initial sense of discomfort or unease. The left brain and right brain are both logical, but the centre of gravity for each logic is different: the left brain is anchored externally (in what we and others think) whereas the right brain is anchored internally (in what we see and what we feel). It makes sense that we can feel slightly disorientated in moving from one mode to the other. (Physically, there is a parallel with switching from 'walking mode' where you lean backwards going down a hill in order to ensure that you don't fall and hurt your head, to 'skiing mode' when you lean forwards going down a hill to keep your skis under control.)

On a personal level, you can experience this discomfort by interlinking your fingers in the 'normal' way. You can then shift your fingers along and see how it feels to have your fingers interlinked in the opposite way. You can do the same exercise by crossing your legs.

This underlying discomfort can make some people very nervous or critical about specific lateral thinking techniques. People will rave about a de Bono lateral thinking course when they are off-site, but when they come back to real work, they will not be confident enough to introduce it into a rationally conditioned work environment. Other people feel patronized when they are asked for their intuitive views of things rather than treated as an expert intellectual. (As one account director in an agency exploded, when he was asked to give his feedback to some new products as part of a new business brainstorm, 'How dare you treat me like a consumer.')

People can feel childish and vulnerable when they are asked to play games or loosen up physically, and this vulnerability can make them sceptical about the use of a technique. Even those people who feel okay about doing intuitive or physical activities can get embarrassed if they feel they are being rationally judged as 'childish' by some of the group sceptics. Physical techniques are particularly vulnerable to left-brain criticism because the left brain judges each separate activity on what it specifically delivers, rather than seeing all activities as working holistically to get the group into a right-brain frame of mind.

Here are a few (some conflicting) ideas on how to minimize discomfort:

- Appeal to the left brain and explain the theory of what you are doing, and why and how exactly each technique is supposed to work on getting you to access your right brain. It might be useful to state clearly that right-brain thinking legitimately helps you to 'see like a child' so that people suffer fewer (negative) side-effects of feeling childish.
- Appeal to the right brain and get participants to be clear about their prejudices/expectations before any given technique. Then get them to observe what happens during the technique and after the technique, and get them to revisit their prejudices/expectations at the end.
- Lead them in gently. Start them on some of the more scientific techniques, then gradually progress them to some of the more intuitive and physical techniques. The advantage here is that the group starts to trust the techniques over time and has the confidence to introduce them with others.
- Plunge them in the deep end. Start them playing the most ridiculous games and creating brand sculptures and allow them to observe how they, and the group, feel and perform in this mode.

Get participants to evaluate what comes out of the session on a practical level (Did we get fresh insights? Did we see new angles on the brand?) and an emotional level (How do I feel about the brand? How do I feel about myself? How do I feel about the rest of the group?). The advantage here is that the group is propelled into a right-brain world that has a strong positive impact on the individual and team building.

A yoga therapist tells an anecdote:

> I recently taught a class of students in wheelchairs… my initial thought
> was to get them to do some gentle stretches with their arms and faces…
> and then I decided instead to ask them to stick their legs straight out and
> hold them there, and if they couldn't physically do that to 'visualize' that
> they were doing it… the exercise built their confidence and meant that
> they pushed themselves harder for the rest of the class.

Self-image

De Bono has found that the single factor that helps determine any individual's creativity is that individual's perception of himself or herself as
'creative'. This creative confidence fuels the person's ability to be creative,
which in turn confirms his or her self-image as creative (see Figure 9.5). An
individual's self-image as 'creative' or as 'non-creative' can equally create
barriers to the complete adoption of creative thinking techniques.

People who believe they are 'creative' sometimes feel that creative
thinking is a unique personal talent. As a result they can resent any techniques that claim to improve their creative thinking, especially if they
view the tools as formulaic and/or they see the people who champion the

Figure 9.5   Virtuous circle of creativity

tools as 'non-creative'. It is almost as though the deliberate decision to be more creative is seen as evidence of left-brain thinking and hence needs to be scorned. As John Hartley, founder of Ascension, says, 'There is sometimes a sense of "gentlemen vs. players" in the UK (brand thinking) fraternity – the "gentlemen" who pride themselves on the effortless nature of their brand thinking and look down on the "players" who have to sweat and toil to get results.'

This same creative self-image can also encourage people to 'mystify' their own thinking process and feel the need to appear to 'pull rabbits out of hats', rather than work in pairs/groups and make the process of thinking transparent. A creative personal image can also be part of a person's 'unique selling proposition' at work, and it can feel as if creative techniques are trying to create a level playing field and hence destroy a person's 'point of difference'.

People who believe that they are 'non-creative' can lack the confidence to try out new techniques. At the same time they quite often are the people who can see the benefits of the techniques (partly because 'creativity' is not intrinsic to their ego). The issue here is that these people quite often lack the creative confidence and/or creative authority to introduce these tools into real work, especially if they get resistance or scepticism from 'creative' people.

Here are some ideas to help break down these barriers:

Give 'creative' people the task of introducing creative techniques in a creative way

Make it a priority on their job spec to try out more creative techniques in their real job but offer scope to design this in a fresh way. Furthermore, encourage them to invent new tools and techniques, and make it a specific part of their job to try these out and report back on what works and what doesn't.

Give 'non-creative' people support in introducing creative techniques into their real job

Again make it part of their job spec to try out more creative thinking techniques in their real job, but offer support from external consultants or internal coaches to give them the confidence to be experimental and the peace of mind to enjoy the benefits of a more right-brain way of working.

The pitch process – an example of breaking down the barriers

Agency people often applaud the pitch process as highly conducive to creative brand thinking. It's interesting to look at how the pitch process breaks down the barriers to creative thinking.

The very fact that both clients and agencies expect fresh brand thinking in a pitch situation seems to allow agencies to push themselves harder and clients to embrace more risk.

Also the pitch seems to act as a 'line in the sand' where the client and incumbent agency can/must renounce 'ownership' for the previous thinking.

Finally people who see themselves as 'creative' are more likely to deliberately try out new creative tools/techniques, because they want to impress the client with their unusual thinking *process* as well as their unusual thinking *results*.

IMPLICATIONS

Commit to the principle of developing creative thinking versus specific techniques

> Part of our job at the forefront of creativity is to encourage risk and failure.
> (Nick Kendall, BBH Group Head of Planning)

If creative thinking is to become part of a group or an individual's day-to-day work, it is important to commit to the principle and deliberately try to break out of our rational conditioning. It is crucial that our intention to think more creatively is not confused with a specific technique that works or doesn't work in a given situation with a given group of people.

It is also important not to limit ourselves to internal meetings and work groups. There is scope to collaborate with consumers and take some risks in the ways we approach research. We might even want to build a sense of experimentation into our commitment, such as, 'This year we'll try out five existing techniques and develop three of our own.'

Apply it on real work NOT just in training sessions

Quite often new techniques are applied with zest on training courses but when we return to work, the barriers of risk and discomfort can mean that we quite often rebound to our left-brain habits. It is important to look at ways to make it easier for people to apply techniques in their job. Only then will people really start to practise them and value them.

Semiotics, the practice of understanding brand norms via looking at the advertising symbolism, was a good example of a new 'right-brain' technique that had a real effect on BT brand thinking because it was used with a real client and real situation.

'Perhaps people could be trained in brand teams or in pairs (account director/account planner) rather than in departments, which would give people some sense of solidarity when they return from training,' suggests Alison Hoad, co-founder of Campbell, Doyle, Dye.

Perhaps you could conduct a live 'test market' by selecting one brand team or account team and challenging them to create a more lateral culture using new techniques. You could then measure their success relative to other teams in terms of the quality of their thinking, their business success and their team morale. It might also be an idea to split the training budget more evenly between off-site and on-site activities, so people can have access to an external resource to help them try out some new techniques or tools.

Reflect your commitment in your structures, rewards and processes

The easiest way to introduce something into a culture is to make it part of the contracts that are in place. If people are hired, assessed and paid on their contributions to right-brain thinking, then people will take it seriously and make it happen. Making it 'part of the job' also helps people get over some of their feelings of fear and discomfort, and in itself can build a counterbalancing feeling of 'ownership' and position it as an opportunity to people with a 'creative' self-image, rather than a threat.

For agencies and consultancies, it might also be a good idea to make it an explicit part of the contract with clients: for example, we will work with you in a way that maximizes all of our right-brain thinking. This overt commitment would then need to be reflected in agency credentials, pitches and client satisfaction studies.

Recruit your future culture

Whether you believe that creative thinkers are born or made, recruiting the 'right' people will be key to any company's success. On one side you can take the view that your primary criterion is 'openness' and seek out people who will be willing to turn their job into a living experiment into new thinking. However, there is a danger here that their 'accepting' natures may limit the boundaries of that thinking. On the other hand you can take the view that inherently 'creative' people will always be one step ahead in this area, and deliberately seek out unconventional thinkers. The danger here is that extreme unconventional thinkers can sometimes lack social skills and be poor team players.

Of course in reality, few people will fit either stereotype and the challenge for a given company will be to create the optimal 'creative culture' to fit their purpose and their vision.

Learn to 'recognize' creative brand thinking

Declan Hogan, founder member of International Brand Architecture, believes that we don't need to do any more creative brand thinking. We just need to recognize it. 'These are the "creative" thoughts that we are discarding at brainstorms as "too mad". These are the "creative" people that we are dismissing because they are too "off the wall".'

It is certainly true that we will need to hone our skills of recognition if we are to embrace a creative brand culture. Hopefully our genuine commitment will take us part of the way there. After that, it is about developing a shared new fluency in right-brain thinking so we can spot ideas that could make a difference.

Keep experimenting

> The big question is no longer if we will fail but how we will fail – the challenge is to 'fail forward' – learn and go on – rather than 'failing backwards' into nostalgia and sentimentalism.
> (Charles Leadbeater)

The techniques and tools for right-brain thinking are supposed to be intuitive, non-linear and subjective, so it makes sense for each group and each person to evolve their own methodologies. There is no hard and fast rule on how this should be done. Our right brains are there but they have been buried underneath the strictures of left-brain thinking. All that is needed now is to start uncovering the capabilities that are inherently ours.

> When I was a child, I spake as a child, I understood as a child, I thought as a child: but when I became a man, I put away childish things. For now we see through a glass, darkly; but then face to face...
> (St Paul, 1 Corinthians 13:11–12)

FURTHER READING

Adams, S (2000) *Dilbert: Random acts of management*, Boxtree

Berger, J (1972) *Ways of Seeing*, Penguin

Bloom, H (2000) *Global Brain*, Wiley

Bogen, J E (1975) Some educational aspects of hemisphere specialisation, *UCLA Educator*, **17**

Boldt, L G (1997) *Zen Soup*, Penguin Arkana

Cooper, R and Sawaf, A (1997) *Executive EQ: Emotional intelligence in business*, Orion Business

Dawkins, R (1989) *The Selfish Gene*, Oxford University Press

de Bono, E (2000) *Six Thinking Hats*, Penguin

De Mello, A (1990) *Awareness*, Fount

Dumas, M and Bloom, B (1999) *Marlene Dumas*, Phaidon

Edwards, E (1993) *Drawing on the Right Side of the Brain*, Harper Collins

Handy, C (1998) *The Hungry Spirit*, Hutchinson Arrow

Institute of Management and Manpower (1998) *Study of UK Corporate Employment Strategies and Trends*, Institute of Management and Manpower

Kaptchuk, E J (1985) *Chinese Medicine: The web that has no weaver*, Rider

Klein, N (2001) *No Logo*, Flamingo

Leadbeater, C (1999) *Living on Thin Air*, Viking
Morgan, A (1999) *Eating the Big Fish*, Wiley
Ridderstrale, J and Nordstrom, K (2000) *Funky Business*, Bookhouse
Russell, B (1998) *The Problems of Philosophy*, Oxford University Press
Saint-Exupéry, A de *The Little Prince*, Heinemann
Schwartz, P (1996) *The Art of the Long View*, Doubleday
Synectics (1993) *Imagine*, Synectics
Trompenaars, F and Hampden-Turner, C (1997) *Riding the Waves of Culture*, Nicholas Brealey
Well, A and Rosen, W (1993) *From Chocolate to Morphine*, Houghton Mifflin

Chapter 10

Adios to the plan: how improvisation and play can help you become more creative

Robert Poynton

Robert Poynton is a recovering account planner. He worked at a number of agencies including BBH and JWT and was one of the founders of the planning consultancy Red Spider. With improviser Gary Hirsch, he founded 'On Your Feet' (improvisation for business) in 1998. On Your Feet works all over the world with clients such as Saatchi & Saatchi, BBDO, Orange, Intel, The

Martin Agency, Wieden and Kennedy, FedEx, Dr. Martens, Will Vinton Studios, Starbucks, the Alliance and Leicester and PricewaterhouseCoopers, as well as the APG on both sides of the Atlantic. For more detail on how these clients have used improvisation see www.on-your-feet.com.

On Your Feet has a sisterly relationship with Adam Morgan and his consultancy eatbigfish. Rob lives in Spain. He is a Fellow of the Royal Society for Arts and a member of Real Madrid Football Club.

THE ONE MINUTE CHAPTER

I often say that nothing is certain. It's a lie, because if nothing else, it's certain that everyone is short of time. So, let me save you 19 minutes, with the one minute version of this chapter.

ONE MINUTE WALTZ

1. The world doesn't go to plan.
2. Plans are clever, abstract and part of the problem.
3. Planning is hooked on cleverness.
4. Planners need to be able to respond creatively to an unpredictable world.
5. Responding creatively is not about clever thinking, it's about what you do.
6. Planners need ways to act creatively (rather than to think creatively).
7. Improvisation is one you can learn.
8. It is based on simple practices.
9. It can be applied to both planners and brands.
10. Improvisers create by:
    - being present;
    - listening;
    - seeing a world full of 'offers' they can use;
    - being prepared to make 'offers' constantly;
    - avoiding blocking;
    - focusing on action (which changes things and creates learning);
    - cutting out activity (stuff that doesn't make a difference);
    - playing with status (what you do, not who you are);
    - ongoing practice (deeper learning not new theories).
11. Agency structures don't help this kind of creativity.
12. Improvisation is not the only answer but it is powerful stuff.

If you are interested in more, read on. If not, sorry about the wasted minute.

ADIOS TO THE PLAN

Welcome to the muddle

My aim in this chapter is to offer a little help to those planners whose world doesn't go to plan. A world where great work dies for the strangest reasons, people crash at least as often as computers and everything happens now (or sooner). A world where nothing is certain and an MBA, lovely though it looks on the CV, is about as useful as a toothpick in a coal-mine. If your world does go to plan – congratulations (or commiserations?) Either way, you can stop here. Otherwise, welcome to the muddle of the universe.

The whole notion of a plan (or strategy) is part of the problem. Plans are about prediction and control. Plans don't allow for human emotions or foibles. And how can you plan for the unexpected? Soldiers know that 'the first casualty of war is the plan'[1] yet planners often cling on to strategy as if it were everything. It isn't. Even Gary Hamel (of *Competing for the Future*, 1996, fame) says that what is important is 'strategizing' – the behaviour that gives rise to strategy, not the strategy itself.[2]

Too clever by half

A strategy is an attempt to order the world. Analysis and reason are used to produce something logical and coherent which gives a feeling of clarity and security. It's clever stuff, but there's a downside. You do this by abstracting, and abstractions distance you from reality.

Planning is hooked on cleverness. Planners are described (in awe) as having 'a brain the size of a planet' as if only the brain counts (what would a planner with a 'heart the size of a planet' be like?) Planning courses teach how to write great briefs, deconstruct competitive advertising or apply a strategic framework. To paraphrase the late George Carman QC, 'the epitaph for planners could be that they give good head'.[3] This isn't wrong, it just isn't enough.

In the real world, if you want people to listen, accept and build on your beautifully crafted words you need more than cleverness. The words alone won't do it, however good they are. You can't create chemistry with people through argument alone, however flawless your logic.

Get out of your head

You have to deal with highly emotional and unpredictable people. So you need to be able to respond spontaneously and creatively as things unfold in a way you didn't plan. Planners need to do this to create relationships, conversations, connections, insights, stories and of course, ideas. Not as a sideshow, but as a central part of the job.

This is not about being clever. In fact, despite the title of this book, it's not about thinking at all. It's what you do that counts, not what you think. Psychologist Mihaly Csikszentmihalyi (who has been studying creativity for 20 years) says, 'Creativity does not happen inside people's heads, but in the interaction between a person's thoughts and a socio-cultural context. It is a systemic rather than an individual phenomenon.'[4]

Responding creatively is about how you act and interact. It requires heart, guts, soul, instinct, intuition, spirit and sensitivity (of all the senses) as well as brains. These things are valued in planners, but not enough. So how can you develop them?

Improv is one way to do this

This chapter is about one way of doing that. Five years ago, I started to use improvisational theatre to get beyond models and frameworks and find new ways to help people act creatively and spontaneously. Improvisation helps you to 'see' reality and then deal with it, rather than trying to control it. It can help you get ideas from your body, generate flow in a conversation or make a whole team creative, not just the people with that label.

I am going to share some of that experience and relate it to planning and brands. Hopefully you will go beyond my suggestions and find your own ways to use it.

Learning to improvise

Let's get one thing straight. Though it comes from the theatre, improvisation is not about being funny on a stage. It is often used to make comedy (most famously on *Whose Line is it Anyway?*) but that is not what it is. Improvisers are just a team of people who work together to create something (in their case a story) to satisfy a customer (in their case an audience) under extreme time pressure (in their case, instantly). Does that sound familiar?

Improvisation does not require genius, telepathy, extraordinary feats of memory or thinking very fast.[5] What improvisers have is a way of working together. They use it to make stories. You can use it to create conversations, meetings, briefings, products, lunch or just about anything. It is more than a technique for brainstorming (though you can use it for that as well). This way of working is based on some simple practices (or behaviours) that enable improvisers to create something out of nothing. These practices can be learned.

So the good news is you can learn to improvise. The bad news is that you can't learn it just by reading a book. I can tell you stories that explain a few of the practices and how others have used them. From there on, it's up to you. You can only really understand it by doing, because this is about behaviour – how you behave and how your brand behaves.

Although each of the practices can be related to both planners and to brands, in each section I have chosen to emphasize one or the other, as follows.

Improv for planners

- Getting fit – being present and listening.
- Seeing a world full of offers.
- Giving offers.
- Co-creating and flow.

Improv for brands

- Action and activity.
- Status.

IMPROV FOR PLANNERS

Getting fit – being present and listening

If you are comfortable in your head, you will need to prepare yourself for getting out of it (as it were). Just as a runner consciously prepares his body for a race, an improviser needs to consciously prepare his or her attitude. That means learning to be 'present' in the moment, attending to what is going on now. Which in turn means listening. You can't be thinking ahead, worrying about something else or fixed on your own ideas. Being present connects you to your context. Without that connection, you are left wandering around in your own head – exactly the place that creativity doesn't happen. How often have you been physically present in a meeting but otherwise absent? As one planner put it, 'Most meetings suck because we decide not to be there.'

What improvisers do is identify what gets in the way of being present and cut it out. Here are three ways to do that.

Focus on other not self

My ego wants me to look good. So I pay most attention to how I appear. Either I get caught up in negative thoughts (such as 'I sound stupid') or I succumb to the desire to impress – and listen only for the chance to advance my pet theory. If I shift focus from my self to the group I become present. (Ironically enough, this also makes you look good to others. So the ego can win too.)

Let go of shadow stories

Shadow stories, full of detail about the way you think things will go, occur instantly, racing ahead of reality. Often I will try and force the conversation to fit my shadow story – which prevents other ideas from being incorporated and other people from being included. Don't try to stop shadow stories coming (you can't) – aim to let them go.[6] This allows your expectation to be constantly revised and fluid. It keeps you open to other people and possibilities.

See beyond private barriers

We normally listen with prejudice. We construct 'private barriers'[7] to confirm our preconceptions. What we hear is tainted by our view of who says it: for example, 'Bill's a nerd, he could never say anything original.'[8] The practice is to replace this 'already listening' with listening in the present moment. To do so you have to slow down.

The thinking part of us fuels these errors – it takes us out of the moment, fast. To put it brutally, my advice is 'stop thinking, start noticing'. This is the most basic lesson from improv – deal with what there IS, not with what there has been, might be, or what you want there to be. You will find that 'intelligence increases when you think less'.[9]

Being present means listening, and listening has many benefits. If you listen people will want to work with you. When people feel heard they express themselves better. A virtuous circle is created where good listening leads to more articulate speech which is easier to listen to. One person can trigger off this reaction. What would meetings be like if everyone listened?

The contribution listening makes is often overlooked, there is so much pressure to speak. Yet speaking takes time from others, while listening creates it.[10] No wonder listening helps relationships.

Listening is crucial for brands too. Do brands really listen to consumers or do they just see them as a means to an end? What effect would it have if a brand paid as much attention to how it listens as to how it speaks? What would brands be like if they listened beyond what they wanted to hear? And if you listen, you never know what you might hear. As one of our workshop participants put it, 'There's free stuff everywhere if you just listen for it.' Free stuff that improvisers call 'offers'.

Seeing a world full of offers

To an improviser the world is full of offers. An actor opens an imaginary door – that's an offer. 'Mum, look', says the second actor, making two more offers simultaneously (that the first actor is his mother and that there is something to look at). Bingo, from nothing you have the beginnings of a story.

An improviser sees everything as an 'offer' he or she can do something with, not as a problem to get rid of. Anything and everything is an offer. You might think this definition is so broad that it's meaningless. In fact, it is the very breadth of the term that makes it so useful. A deadline is an offer. Someone falling asleep in your presentation is an offer. A budget cut is an offer. A creative grilling your brief is an offer.

To see everything as an offer is a basic practice of improvisation. This shift of attitude is interesting. As soon as I see something as an offer, it becomes one. You don't judge things as good or bad, you just look for how to use what you are presented with. Everything becomes something to work with.

A few months ago I met the head of training of a New York agency. I sent her a brochure in advance. When I arrived she said, 'I didn't understand your material.' 'Great,' I said. She was incredulous. 'You're happy about that?' I explained, 'I said "Great" because I saw your comment as an offer, and now I know what to do – explain. Which is better than beating myself up or trying to defend the brochure.'

Someone fell asleep in a workshop. I could feel my mind collecting the bricks to build a paralysing wall of judgement: 'He must be bored, they are all bored, everyone hates this, the workshop is a failure, they hate me.' The speed with which my mind does this is very unhelpful.

Making an effort of will, I chose to see 'Bill asleep' as an offer. I found this liberating. I could choose what to do. I could talk in a whisper (making a joke at Bill's expense), ask if they were all bored or, as I actually did, clap to punctuate my speech and wake Bill up. Seeing everything as an offer is a powerful practice. And it's only half of the story.

Giving offers

To give an offer is an act of generosity. This isn't altruism, it's effective teamwork. Who would you rather be around – someone who is generous, or someone who isn't? Making more offers will make you better to work with. And that small change will make a difference to the relationships that fuel a creative process.

A planner working as a consultant for a client (who was also a friend) became frustrated because she felt that all her ideas were turned down. The relationship (professional and personal) suffered. Reflecting on it, the planner realized that the client paid her to make offers. So she stopped draining her energy through worrying and channelled it into making more offers. This enabled her to change the relationship for the better without having to confront the client.

When you brief creatives you are giving an offer. They are unlikely to agree instantly with your brief. Be willing to make your offer in different ways, instead of being stuck on how you have written it down. Notice the offers they make back and use them. For example, if they say it's boring, see that as an offer. Make the brief into a story, or explain why it's interesting to the target, or give them some context, or ask them which is the least (or most) boring part, or open up to the possibility that they might be right and ask them how to stop it being so boring. Use their offer and look for one of the many possible offers you could make back. Whatever you do, don't block them by telling them it is NOT boring.

If you think of a brief as an 'offer' you jettison a lot of baggage. It's less about getting it right and more about getting going. You and your brief become more inviting, more open, less onerous. An 'offer' is so obviously a start point, which is what a brief should be.

Making an offer feels like a risk because it might be rejected, but if you make no offers you have zero capacity to create change or action, which is a much bigger risk.

Examine the offers a brand makes – could it make different offers? Ask, 'What is the offer at the heart of the brand?' This simple question gets beyond the jargon of planning and marketing. You are more likely to get a deep, emotional answer than a clever, technical one. For example, Adam Morgan says that the offer at the heart of Apple is Steve Job's assertion that 'people with passion can change the world for the better'.[11]

A planner's job is all about seeing and making offers. You look for offers in the market, the brand, the product, the consumer and so on. You make offers to creatives (a brief), which the agency turns into offers to a client (the work), whose business is to make offers to a consumer (the brand). When everything seems too complex, too fast moving or too difficult, just ask, which offers can you use and what offers can you make? All you need is to link a few offers together and you have the beginnings of a story.

Co-creating and flow

Claire Hassid of Saatchi & Saatchi New York (currently planning director, but previously a creative director) has this to say on how we come up with ideas:

> It's about making leaps of logic between things that were not connected before. Leaping requires agility of the mind. It's hard to do if you are not flexible, imaginative, and free (here's the odd part) *in both mind and body* [italics added]. One's whole being has to be kind of loose to be a great ideas person. Fearlessness helps too. What's great about improv is that it teaches you how to flow with ideas. It keeps mind and body loose and lets you have fun. It allows other people to join in the fun and makes ideas travel to their most logical place.

So creativity comes from connecting.[12] More than a mental activity, it is an emotional and bodily state of being 'loose', fearless, and having fun.[13] And without flow you aren't going anywhere, let alone somewhere new. Flow is fundamental to all creative processes.[14]

Improvisers have a disarmingly simple way of connecting offers to create flow. By being present they attend to the offers around them. Then they just 'accept' one of these offers and use it, ideally giving another offer back (for someone else to use). At its simplest, that's all they do. For example, Geoff mimes opening a door. Arnold walks through it and says, 'Hello Granny'. Arnold is accepting the offer of the door and using it, creating flow. 'Hello Molly dear,' Geoff replies, accepting the offer and becoming 'Granny'. There are lots of ways the story can go from here as long as the actors give and accept offers that build on what has come before. The commonest way of accepting is to say 'yes'. Accepting and giving an offer back is called 'Yes, and …'.[15]

You can apply this anywhere and everywhere. If you accept the offers around you, from colleagues, clients or consumers, use them and add something to them, you will be able to respond to anything, generate flow and create new possibilities. It's really that simple.

That doesn't make it easy. The opposite of accepting is blocking, and it's everywhere. We all do it more than we think. To block someone is to deny their reality. For example:

Geoff: Hello Mother.
Arnold: I am not your Mother I am a fish.

Geoff feels well and truly shafted. The flow is killed, it is very hard to create anything. When offers are blocked, ideas and relationships lose energy and become negative. The commonest (but by no means the only) form of blocking is saying 'no'.

Improv guru Keith Johnstone sums up the difference between accepting and blocking. He says, 'There are those who prefer to say "yes" and those who prefer to say "no". Those who say "yes" are rewarded by the adventures they have, and those who say "no" are rewarded by the security they attain. There are far more "no" sayers than "yes" sayers.'

Blocking isn't always bad, but it's far too common. And if you are interested in creativity it's adventure you want. As one planning director put it when I asked her what she thought planners could learn from improv, 'Accept, accept, accept'.

IMPROV FOR BRANDS

I said this is about behaviour, so here are some examples of how brands could behave differently.

Action and activity

In stories action occurs when somebody is changed. At the end of the film *American Beauty*, Colonel Fitts tries to kiss Lester Burnham. From this one small movement we realize that he is a repressed homosexual. Learning this changes the whole film, so this is action. Yet all we see is two men standing in a garage.

Contrast that with a Bond film (any Bond film). The car/boat/motorbike/ ski chase starts with Bond ahead of the baddies, and ends with Bond ahead of the baddies. A lot has happened but nothing has changed. Expensive special effects notwithstanding, this is activity, not action. Hollywood should re-name the genre, Activity Movies.

Action creates characters, stories and brands. Yet activity is what you normally get. Plans are full of 'marketing activity', which is exactly what it is – stuff that doesn't make a difference. Creating action means working less (which is harder than it sounds). If you can't be sure something will make a difference, don't do it. Write yourself a list of things not to do. The longer the better. When you stop doing things which don't make a difference, you have more time and energy to commit to the things that do. In *Eating the Big Fish* (1999) Adam Morgan calls this 'sacrifice'. There is plenty of 'activity' to sacrifice – audiences, media, product lines, messages, take your pick.

What else can you do to create action? Improvisers do things to advance the story. They learn not to confuse 'stuff happening' with action. Try this. Scrutinize all of your brand's activity for the last year. Did it make a difference; is it activity or action?[16] If you can't tell, then it's activity, by definition. Apply that knowledge to this year's work – and cut out the activity.

If a story gets stuck, an improviser will make an offer that ensures somebody learns something ('Dad, I'm pregnant'). Where or how could your brand create learning?

Improvisers also break routines. A routine is a pattern of behaviour. Breaking the routine creates action (for example, the routine of waiting for a bus is broken by the bus arriving). Look for routines in anything and everything the brand does. List them, without judging them. Then choose the ones you think could usefully be broken, and brainstorm ways to break them.

A client I know spotted that most meetings are activity. She decided, as a policy, to only attend meetings where her presence made a difference. She wouldn't attend to show her face or keep someone else happy. Half her meetings disappeared. Six months later I asked her what effect cutting these meetings out had had. 'None', she said – proof that they were activity.

Status

Keith Johnstone observes that 'every inflection and movement implies a status'. Johnstone is interested in making scenes 'authentic'. You can use it to do the same for brands. Status is being played all the time, whether the players realize it or not. Brands play a certain status (high or low) to consumers in every interaction (and vice versa).

Improvisers know that status shifts engage an audience. For example, a traffic cop we expect to be high status plays low status and apologizes to a speeder for stopping him. Audiences love this.

The same is true for a brand. Airlines normally play high status. We want them to – we pay them large amounts of money and put our lives in their hands. And the pilot is meant to know where the plane is. A few years ago I was on a United Airlines flight to San Francisco when the pilot announced, 'Those of you on the left of the plane can see Yosemite. At

least, I hope it's Yosemite, because if it's not, we're lost.' This pilot deliberately lowered his status and that of the brand, and in so doing made me feel more warmly towards United. This was a creative thing to do. He humanized the brand and punctured the remoteness that comes with playing high status relentlessly. The humour came from shifting the status the pilot and the brand normally play.

Here's an example of the opposite shift – from low to high status. Body Shop packaging is low status (plain ordinary bottles). The luscious ingredients fetched from exotic foreign lands via a fair trade policy are high status. As you open the bottle there is a transition from low to high status. If the packaging were high status as well it wouldn't have the same impact.

The point here is not that low or high status is good. The idea is to use shifts in status to be creative. A change in status is action. The practice is to notice status and play around with it. This can get you out of the straightjacket of a brand definition, without throwing away consistency. Status shifts give you a way to modulate who you are while still being recognizably the same. Be the same character, but play a different status.

Shifting status is useful on a personal level as well. For example, planners who normally play low status before feisty (high status) creatives, would do well to play high status occasionally. Or vice versa: a brain-the-size-of-a-planet (high status) planner might enhance a relationship by admitting ignorance (playing low status) on some subjects.

This is harder than it seems because each of us are good at playing a particular status. (This is true for brands also.) First we get comfortable, then we get stuck. Try noticing your own natural tendency and find (safe) opportunities to play the opposite. How you use your body is crucial. To play high status, keep your head still (don't change anything else). To play low status move your head around.[17] At the moment I am practising high status on waiters (you have to start somewhere).

A FINAL THOUGHT – ABOUT PRACTICE

There are more practices than space to write about them, so I would like to end with a point about practice in general. Practices are something you do. Knowing what they are is not enough, you have to use them. Moreover, to practise something you keep doing it; in different situations, with different people. You are never 'done' (you can't be too good at listening). Through practice you create new ability. Practice is itself creative.

I have been practising 'accepting' for nearly five years. Maybe I am slow but I find this reassuring. A simple practice, which continues to help me learn, is an antidote to stress. I feel less pressure to keep up with shiny new theories. Instead I get more from what I already know.

It takes a considerable effort of will to practise. Starting small helps. Choose something that attracts your interest and a specific situation to apply it. For example, take something difficult and look at it as an offer. Do this for a while and see where it gets you. If it helps, you will find other ways to extend the practice. If it doesn't, let it go. Often these things lie dormant until an appropriate stimulus crops up. Either that, or you could go and sign up for an MBA now.

Breaking barren ground

An advertising agency is not an easy place to become more creative. The biggest barrier is the 'creative' department. Not the people in it, but the fact that it exists, the structure. The implication is that creativity resides there. To an improviser the idea of putting creativity in a department of its own is simply bizarre.[18]

Planners are in an interesting position. Sitting between creatives, consumers and clients they have the opportunity to break this structure and make everyone more creative. To do so, they need to get out of their own intellectual straightjacket with its emphasis on cleverness, abstraction and thought. In my experience great planners do this. By nature they are improvisers. They listen well, see and make offers all the time, accept ideas from anywhere, don't block, create flow, focus on action not activity, shift their status and so on. They also tend to be playful. And these extra qualities are what make them stand out, not their cleverness.

The trouble with improv as a method is that it's fun. 'No pain, no gain' has been seared so deeply on our consciousness that anything enjoyable is often dismissed as trivial. It's not. Improvisation is a way to learn some powerful stuff. One way, not the only way – you shouldn't treat improv with reverence. We can all do it. It has been developed through use (and mis-use). So take what is here as an offer, and add to it, re-combine it, mix it, 'Yes-and' it but above all use it, rather than think about it. And I would love to hear how you get on. You can reach me at rob@on-your-feet.com.

ACKNOWLEDGEMENTS

I am conscious of the irony involved in writing about an experiential method like improvisation. But this chapter is grounded in experience gleaned from many workshops, so thanks to all the planners who have worked with On Your Feet for their help – whether conscious or unconscious. Special thanks to Jane Cantellow, Karen Hand, Bill Ward and Kathy Oldridge for coming out to play as part of the development of this chapter. To Adam Morgan for constant guidance and classical wisdom. To Claire Hassid, Caley Shaffer, Vicente Valjalo, Paul Neal and many others for their fantastic suggestions via e-mail.

I owe huge debts to Keith Johnstone whose work has inspired way beyond the theatre, and of course to Gary Hirsch, companion in the adventure that is On Your Feet and illustrator of this chapter. And for teaching me all about improvisation in life to Bruno, Mateo and Beatriz.

I make one claim to originality in this chapter – the mistakes. They are all mine.

NOTES

1 As I heard it. Norman Schwarzkopf said this, though who knows which famous general said it first.
2 See his paper 'The search for strategy' or check out strategosnet.com.
3 Carman was talking about actress Gillian Taylforth of East Enders during a libel case.
4 Based on an in-depth study of great living creators.
5 Sincere apologies to all those improvisers I have worked with for blowing the gaff.
6 In his fabulous book *Out of Control* (1994), Kevin Kelly suggests that 'letting go, with dignity' is the 'chief psychological chore of the 21st century'.
7 John Steinbeck and Edward F. Ricketts, *The Sea of Cortez*, quoted in *Improvisation Inc.* (2000) by Robert Lowe.
8 Psychologists call this 'labelling theory'. In essence it means that if you label something, your perception will then tend to select the data that confirm, rather than challenge that label.
9 This is the subtitle of Guy Claxton's book *Hare Brain, Tortoise Mind* (1998), which gives a very robust explanation of why thinking less helps.
10 For this and other wonderful thoughts about time see Jay Griffith's brilliant book *Pip Pip* (2000).
11 Consultant, author of *Eating the Big Fish* (1999) and erstwhile planning director of TBWA Chiat Day in Los Angeles.
12 This is widely accepted. See Jack Foster (1996), *How to Get Ideas*.
13 Neither Claire nor I mean to suggest that you have to be an athlete, just that you need to involve all of you, and your body is a significant part of that. You forget it and all the senses it has at your peril.
14 See Mihaly Csikszentmihalyi's books *Creativity* (1997) and *Flow* (1992). He believes flow underlies both creativity and 'optimal experience'. In other words, it doesn't just make you creative, it makes you happy. That's encouraging.
15 In business, 'Yes but ...' is far more common than 'Yes and...'.
16 This is similar to an exercise called Picasso described in *Eating the Big Fish* by Adam Morgan (1999).
17 Strange though this sounds the effect is quite amazing; it even works on the telephone. For more on this see Keith Johnstone's books *Impro* (1981) and *Impro for Storytellers* (1999) (pp 33 and 219 respectively).
18 My partner Gary Hirsch has said as much to a number of agencies, bless him.

REFERENCES

Claxton, G (1998) *Hare Brain, Tortoise Mind*, Fourth Estate. *Robust scientific explanations of why thinking less increases your intelligence. Really.*

Csikszentmihalyi, M (1992) *Flow: The psychology of happiness*, Rider

Csikszentmihalyi, M (1997) *Creativity: Flow and the psychology of discovery and invention*, Perennial (Harper Collins). *Fascinating and inspiring studies of creativity and its relationship to happiness.*

Foster, J (1996) *How to Get Ideas*, Berrett-Koehler. *Ex agency creative explains where ideas come from.*

Griffiths, J (2000) *Pip Pip: A sideways look at time*, Flamingo. *Fascinating ruminations on time.*

Johnstone, K (1981) *Impro*, Methuen

Johnstone, K (1999) *Impro for Storytellers*, Faber and Faber. *Classic improv texts.*

Kelly, K (1994) *Out of Control: The biology of machines*, Fourth Estate. *Complexity, ecology, creativity, the evolution of evolution, Borgian Libraries and warring robots. It's all here.*

Lowe, R (2000) *Improvisation Inc.*, Jossey Bass Wiley. *Another take on improv in business to contrast with mine.*

Morgan, A (1999) *Eating the Big Fish*, Wiley. *Study of challenger brands.*

FURTHER READING

Hamel, G and Prahalad, C K (1996) *Competing for the Future*, Harvard Business School Press

Pert, C (1999) *Molecules of Emotion*, Pocket Books. *Scientific underpinnings of emotion and a new understanding of the relationship between mind and body by the discoverer of endorphins.*

Chapter 11

Lest we forget: homage to some old brand thinking

Merry Baskin

Merry's resume reads like a steamer trunk with career enhancing stints in London, Paris, New York, Stockholm, and Brussels. (Had she stuck to the first three she could have launched her own fashion house!) Instead, after several years as one of the industry's top planning directors (including running the UK's largest planning department at JWT and America's coolest at Chiat/Day), she founded her own strategic planning consultancy, Baskin Shark (where brands move forward or die!), in 2000. She is also a partner in

Express Train, a group providing training for the advertising and marketing industry.

With planning proteges all over the world, she remains one of the leading lights behind the renaissance and expansion of the APG (UK Chairman 1998–2000); winner of two consecutive IPA Advertising Effectiveness awards 1996/1998, the MRS/ISBA best paper 2001 and several US Effies (1986/ 1997/1988); contributor to the APG book How to Plan Advertising; *author of a revised millennium definition of Account Planning, and a witty and astute speaker on many industry conference platforms.*

For further details on her other published pieces and activities, contact www.baskinshark.com and for information on training, go to www.express-train.co.uk.

Otherwise you can find her digging on her organic allotment in Gloucestershire.

INTRODUCTION

In a book filled with new, radical thinking about brands from a bunch of comparative youngsters, I wanted to end with a nod to the sanity and intelligence of the older generation. After all, a lot of the original and early thinking about brands has stood commerce in pretty good stead for a great many years. I should add that the majority of this cadre are still going strong and continuing to spout forth original thoughts from their well-earned lofty positions of authority, Wendy Gordon's chapter in this very book being a case in point. I make no apology for the somewhat demotic delivery that follows.

There are many original pearls of wisdom lying around out there that I passionately believe we would be foolish to discard and extremely stupid to ignore, despite all this 'brand new thinking'. The following (distilled) insights or observations about brands and brand communications are, I believe, the b(l)inding truths to which we should all adhere as the business in which we operate becomes more complex, the money at stake spirals and the pace of change accelerates into hyperspace.

For me, these basic tenets represent the top five things 'I wish I had known about brands and advertising when I was 25'. (Sadly, for both myself and my clients at the time, I didn't.) I now find myself still applying and explaining these fundamentals in my business efforts every day, because there now appears to be an emergent generation of Gonzo marketers and planners who haven't got a clue, and are not particularly interested in finding one.

In most instances, these aphorisms are powerful glimpses lifted from much deeper thinking and gleaned from a wider expertise which is better expressed and elaborated on in the original extensive treatises on the subject. (See the list of full papers/books at the end of this chapter.) But in this day and age of 'small is better', 'less is more' and 'attention deficit disorder', I have summarized short out-takes that have been useful to me as pithy *aides-mémoire* but are actually poor relations to the complicated truth they hint at. The best thing you can do, if they strike a chord, is to look up the paper or publication itself and devour every word.

The five areas of insight can be summarized as:

- Brands are a lot more complex than some brand experts or various and sundry brand management tools would have you believe.

- Like a shark, brands must move forward or die. Brands need to be future oriented, rather than dwell on their past.
- We don't spend nearly enough time thinking about how communication works, and this gets us into all sorts of trouble.
- The truth about advertising (in particular) is that it works in lots of different ways.
- Market research is important to brand understanding, but techniques have always been theoretically weak – beware!

BRANDS ARE A LOT MORE COMPLEX THAN SOME BRAND EXPERTS OR VARIOUS AND SUNDRY BRAND MANAGEMENT TOOLS WOULD HAVE YOU BELIEVE

The first big thought to get your head around is that brands exist in people's heads, not in reality:

> The way people build brands in their heads... is an intensely creative process. We build an image as birds build nests – from scraps and straws we chance upon... Once we understand that everyone creates their own brands in their own heads in their own way, we're half way to sanity.
> (Jeremy Bullmore)

> The brand is simply a collection of perceptions in the mind of the consumer.
> (Paul Feldwick)

Here's a rare thing – a brand 'owner' who gets this, apparently:

> Brands exist because people want them to exist... brands ultimately belong to consumers. It is people who call brands into existence – who form attachments, detest homogeneity, value consistency and delight in conferring personality characteristics on animals, entities and inanimate objects.
> (Niall FitzGerald, CEO, Unilever PLC)

Presumably that's why he recently chose to axe Unilever's brand portfolio from 1600 to 400 'power brands' by 2004 – they had no consumer calling – although some might argue Unilever's problems lie with owning too many brands in a globalizing management system that stifles their potential, rather than consumers getting tired of them. Perhaps better to look to 3M who also reduced their brand portfolio from 1,500 to 700 in two years, but in addition cut down the creation of new brands in one year from 73 to 4, which enabled them to grow the existing brands through renewal rather than (costly) brand new brand launches.

This leads me on to an important sub-point, namely that brand managers don't manage brands, consumers do. The concept of brand management ('the managing directors of the products', as Procter & Gamble originally coined them) is an oxymoron. You (the brand owner) can't control it. They (the brand's customers) do. The power to make or break a brand's success lies with its public and how that public responds to the brand in all its manifestations. The best that marketers can hope for is to understand their customer well enough to be able to put out the right sort of stimulus for them to respond to. A founder's dream or philosophy may have conceived the brand in the first place (think Steve Jobs and Apple), but once it is out there, it belongs to the buyer or user.

> A product is an objective thing; and a brand is one person's individual and subjective summary of all the satisfactions that product supplies. No two people will see it in exactly the same way.
> (Jeremy Bullmore)

However, and here's the rub, most brands (unless perhaps they are 'cult' brands) are simply not as important to their consumers' lives as they are to their brand owners. So for me, the issue is one of perspective. Never delude yourself that you can control or manage your brand's image. Change the business cards from 'brand manager' to 'blender of some of the brand stimuli that make up a brand's character'. Stop setting unrealistic image or attribute objectives for your brand tracking research to pick up, and talking in meetings like some overweening brand despot.

> Impressions of brands are built up over time through a series of individual tiny signals, generally including product experience.... Each time someone sees any kind of ad, promotion, show-card, editorial or review

for your brand, each time someone uses it or talks to someone else about it, they are receiving another small stimulus. Individuals are rarely aware … where a particular impression has come from.… The brand slowly develops a personality, the size and shape of which is moulded organically by these stimuli.
(Alan Hedges, 1974)

Brand communications are in a sense mosaics of meaning. Consumers form impressions of the brand, the single brand, the family of brands, the company brand, from many different places.
(Judie Lannon)

This brings me on to the subject of product versus brand. Almost 30 years ago in his book *Developing New Brands* (1977), Stephen King wrote the immortal and oft cited words 'A product is something that is made, in a factory; a brand is something that is bought, by a customer.' (Note the punctuation, please, if you are going to re-quote this.)

In actuality, 20 years before in 1955, Gardner and Levy were among the first to articulate the difference between the brand and the product, and to grasp the fact that it lies not simply in 'brand facts', *per se*, but in 'sets of ideas, feelings and attitudes that consumers have about brands'. Emotional ties, in other words, are, like all relationships, very difficult to pin down.

Another aspect that distinguishes a brand from its product counterpart is fame. It is very important to distinguish brand fame from familiarity and reputation (the usual means of justifying the role of brands).

Identity… is basically what distinguishes branded from unbranded products. It is what enables people to handle brands easily in their minds. If we have a clear picture of a brand in our minds to refer to we can handle it easily in decision making, even at our lower levels of consciousness. We have the reassurance that comes with familiarity.
(Alan Hedges, 1974).

But FAME is the really valuable thing. The concept of brand fame is a Jeremy Bullmore-ism:

We value the famous far more than the little known… just about the only thing successful brands have in common is a kind of fame. Fame lends a certain value to things and to people. Famous things can be shared, referred to, laughed about. Famous things are literally a talking point.

Why is fame important? If only a small percentage of the population can afford to buy a Patek Philippe watch, why advertise in mainstream media to everyone? The obvious answer is the self-expression one – that what is the point in a customer spending tens of thousands of pounds on a watch if no one is going to know how successful that means he or she is? But Patek Philippe isn't just famous for its price, it is also famous for its unparalleled Swiss workmanship. So the second key lesson here is that you have to be famous for something. (I was going to use Rolex as an example here, but that great brand is now becoming famous for something else, which is most unfortunate.)

Many people are marching up to podia and pronouncing in 'new news' style that the corporate brand is increasingly important and will ultimately overtake the individual brand in the pantheon. All well and good, but in fact what we have here is another piece of brand foresight that originated from the pen of Stephen King:

> The emphasis is going to have to be more firmly on company as brand or on families of brands. If individual lines can be quickly copied then it will be the reputation of the maker that matters. Marketing companies will increasingly recognize that their main unique asset is as much who they are as what they make.
>
> (Stephen King, *Developing New Brands*, introduction to 1984 edition)

He went on to elaborate on this theme in a seminal paper in 1991. He identifies six seismic forces driving this shift, three from the consumer and three from the corporation. Two of the most influential, to my mind, are the explosion of individual customer data and the constant round of mergers and acquisitions, restructuring and unbundling of companies (think of the financial sector). The former means having unprecedented (swamping?) levels of consumer understanding; the latter means no longer knowing who you are, who you work for and what the company stands for (this week). A potentially lethal cocktail for brand health.

Many have argued that Naomi Klein's *No Logo* (2001) is in fact not about brands, but about the ethos of companies and the growing interest consumers are taking in the company behind the brand. For the bigger and more famous these companies and their brands become, the more vulnerable they are if they are not ethical or environmentally sound. Despite her best efforts to turn brands into the Bad Guys, let's not forget that brands originated not as a form of exploitation of a gullible public but as a form of consumer protection; a guarantee of authenticity, of consistency. A benefit people were and are prepared to pay for, so the brand is not just of value to the corporate brand owner, natch. However, it seems only fair that the brand owner also has to keep its nose clean, in this media savvy, Big Brother world, if only to ensure the brand's good reputation.

> It may have been possible, not so long ago, for a brand to live a life securely ring fenced from its corporate owners. Few members of the public knew the name of its manufacturer; even fewer allowed their view of that manufacturer to affect their view of the brand. Today, no brand enjoys such immunity.
> (Niall Fitzgerald, 2001)

Add to this confusion the fact that most brands are no longer simply products, but a combination of products and services. Even an FMCG brand like Persil has a clothes care line. British Gas has a credit card called Goldfish that (among other things) will let you borrow money and use points to pay your gas bill. The traditional primary brand contacts of consumer and retailer find themselves multiplied tenfold to encompass myriad different constituencies; employees, distributors, shareholders, trades unions, pressure groups, journalists, the City, the government and so on. And each of those contact points uses different media and a different method to communicate.

Despite these seismic changes and this increased complexity, I believe the same rules for brand success outlined by these experts still apply, and to ignore those rules can lead to very expensive mistakes.

Moreover, all those brand management frameworks, purporting to offer the key to successful brand management, these terribly clever models of thinking, from the 'brand onion' to the 'brand wheel' to the 'brand funnel' to the 'brand terrapin' (OK I made that last one up) are actually an unhelpful illusion. They give the impression that they can provide a framework to manage the multi-faceted nature of the brand. However fancy they are, they simply cannot deal with the complexity, nor can they predict what the competition will do, nor how the consumer will respond.

To summarize this section, brand building is a complicated task, and the best we can hope for, as Bullmore puts it, is 'to provide some of the raw materials from which brands are built', to get them into people's hearts and minds, to make our brand famous FOR something. Talkability, or what researchers might excruciatingly call '...is a popular brand nowadays' is what we are striving for.

LIKE A SHARK, BRANDS MUST MOVE FORWARD OR DIE. BRANDS NEED TO BE FUTURE ORIENTED, NOT DWELLING ON THEIR PAST

The identity of a brand, as already pointed out, is built by consumers from lots of different bits and pieces and lives inside their minds. Said brand may well have started out as one (wo)man's passion, and that person's original idea or vision may well still reside at the heart of the brand – as in Anita Roddick and Body Shop – but while a brand's image may be fairly stable, it is not a constant. As the stimuli about a brand changes, through use, mis-use, abuse or lack of use, so does the consumer's opinion of the brand evolve. Because the world around us is in a state of constant flux, it is actually impossible for a brand to remain static; it can however, stagnate, and get left behind.

Think of the challenge facing Levi's – a youth brand that needs to recruit new teenagers to its franchise every year, while some of its older customers, a whole generation of (now) big-bottomed baby boomers, insist on still wearing them into their 50s. Not to mention what the fashion market is saying about jeans and denim, or what their competition is up to (or even who their competition is), or technology making new advances, or new distribution channels opening up, and so on. For all these reasons, standing still is simply not an option. Savvy brand owners are very keen to keep the brand's image and functionality up with the times:

> The size of the reservoir (of consumer predisposition toward the brand) depends on the distinctiveness, the relevance, the fundamental usefulness of the brand to the consumer, and then of the ability of management to keep the reservoir topped up with relevant innovation and flowing freely. (Niall Fitzgerald, 2001)

But this is not as easy as it sounds. Just as it is almost impossible for a brand to be all things to all people, to sell itself to everyone, so it is tough for one brand to satisfy one person throughout life. For consumers themselves change; they get older, their lifestyle changes, their bank balance waxes and wanes, they move house, they have kids – all these will impact how they feel about and use certain brands. Something to bear in mind, however, is that this does happen quite slowly, almost imperceptibly, and it always has:

> The ideas people have about (a reputable brand) are not completely malleable, not idly swayed by one communication and then another. If the public believes that a certain brand is of inferior quality or that another 'is on the skids', or that some other has all the latest improvements, those beliefs are not usually modified very rapidly. Such reputations are built through time, frequently in ways management is not aware of.
> (Gardner and Levy, 1955)

Clearly Gerald Ratner and his Marks & Spencer prawn sandwich remark to the City which seemed to bankrupt his company overnight is a recent exception to this 'rule' laid down all those years ago. But what Gardner and Levy say goes some way to explain why brand image tracking drifts so slowly over time. Despite the best intentions of various brand communications designed to 'tell' consumers lots of different messages, emanating from multiple different copy strategies, launched by the ever changing guard of brand managers (new ones on average every 18 months now, apparently), it just doesn't work like that.

WE DON'T SPEND NEARLY ENOUGH TIME THINKING ABOUT HOW COMMUNICATION WORKS AND THIS GETS US INTO ALL SORTS OF TROUBLE

There are a variety of reasons why people don't think enough about how communications work. For starters, because it works in many different ways, and each instance is different depending on the circumstances. So there are no short cuts, no single technique that tells us how it does.

Maybe we think we do know how it works and go about our lives with certain rules set down in our heads. This may be fine, until things start to get tricky. This is true, of course, not just for advertising but all forms of brand communication.

How often at the outset of a relationship between a new client and a communications agency (before there is even any creative work to argue about) do they ask each other for their theory of how communication works? Does either of them even subscribe to one? What do they believe the role of each medium is? Do they differentiate between long-term and short-term effects? Does either party believe that there is one piece of research that can predict whether or not the idea will work when it is exposed? And so on. Try my handy quiz to see what you believe (focusing on advertising here, still the bulk of most marketing budgets).

COSMO-style quiz for advertising theory

I BELIEVE THAT:	Agree	Disagree	Don't know or care
The sole job of advertising is to sell the most goods the quickest	1	2	3
It is possible to gauge an ad's potential effectiveness based on one exposure	1	2	3
An ad works on the mind in a sequence; I see it, I register it, I understand it, I accept what it is saying, then I act upon it	1	2	3
Advertising works in the mind at the conscious and rational level	1	2	3
Words/verbal messages are more powerful than pictures in communication	1	2	3
Asking people questions about their opinions does not affect their responses	1	2	3
A good advert is one people can remember (often as much as three days after seeing it)	1	2	3
You can measure how well an ad is branded by asking consumers if it 'could it be an ad for something else?'	1	2	3
You can tell if an ad is well branded by the number of times the brand name is mentioned in the ad	1	2	3
It is unnecessary to read Alan Hedges' book *Testing to Destruction* (1974) before buying or using any pre-testing methodologies	1	2	3

ANSWER: Mostly 1's – you are a(n) (American) client or a researcher with a template to sell; mostly 2's – you must be a top planner in a (British) advertising agency; mostly 3's – why are you reading this chapter?

Perhaps you or your client do have a theory and you believe (as Jeremy Bullmore so amusingly described it) 'that the only true paradigm for advertising is the high performance brain invader, by which something called a proposition is rifled repetitively into consumers' heads until they can play it back flawlessly to day-after recallers?'

This may seem a wantonly simplistic and naïve view of how advertising works, or a particularly cruel caricature of clients, but I have sat in on those ad tracking debrief meetings where the only response deemed worth anything is whether or not consumers (spontaneously) remembered seeing the ad on television, whether they could play back the slogan, and how many boxes were shifted during that correlating week the ad was on air. If only it were that easy.

So how do you avoid falling into this trap? I firmly believe you've got to have a theory or an idea before you start.

> We will never use research to the full unless we start from a carefully worked out theory of what the brand is, why it is successful or not, and what advertising can contribute.
> (Stephen King)

Why does Stephen say you need a theory? There are several facets to the answer: the usefulness of a theory, any theory, in and of itself, acts as a marker in the sand from which hypotheses can spring. Second, the fact that it is a theory and not a 'golden rule' or a statement of fact or a piece of incontrovertible proof – because, with a few exceptions, measuring or predicting communication performance in isolation is almost impossible. This means that judgement and thinking comes to the fore, pushing out that dread word 'test'. Thirdly, the complexity of the human mind, and the unpredictability of markets mean that while there is no single formulaic process for perfect results every time, there is always a need for illumination and an opportunity for learning about said theory.

> Kurt Lewin said that there was nothing so practical as a good theory. He was right. Knowing why or how something works facilitates the transfer of experience. Knowing how advertising works helps brief the agency, helps share experience and provides measures of performance and diagnostics when things go wrong. Knowing how advertising works illuminates both the possible and the improbable. Advertisers need to have

some idea of how their advertising works in order to understand roughly what change can be expected at what cost.
(Tim Ambler, in Ambler and Vakratsas, 1998)

Your theory of how the piece of communication will work should of course be intrinsically linked to the objectives you set it. Having an idea of how it is going to work against its target audience is, I firmly believe, one of the key jobs of the account planner.

Given that the effects of advertising campaigns are so difficult to measure, a good planner, I would posit, 'builds up a body of principles, an increased understanding of audience composition and reactions, and a wide-ranging familiarity with procedures and techniques, plus a sense of responsibility and pride in good performance'. Actually that was written in 1955 by Gardner and Levy, and was referring to the role of standards within an advertising agency, but in today's world, I take it to mean the planner. Let's not forget that the account planning job function was originally conceived as a way of 'dealing with' market research:

> It seemed wrong to me that it should be the account man who decided what data should be applied to ad planning and whether or not a researcher was needed. Partly because account men were rarely competent to do this – but more dangerously because my own account man experience had shown – clients on the one hand and creative director on the other made one permanently tempted to be expedient. Too much data could be uncomfortable. I decided therefore that a trained researcher should be put alongside the account man on every account. He should be there as of right, with equal status as a working partner.
> (Stanley Pollitt, How I started account planning in agencies, *Campaign*, April 1979)

Unfortunately, too many planners have now lost their rigour and objectivity and become 'shrills' for the work, browbeaten by underperforming creative directors into defending mediocre ideas, or too busy or too clueless or too intellectually lazy to figure out how or why or what effects a campaign or execution might have in the marketplace.

Having started out as a graduate trainee at BMRB, then a research company subsidiary of J Walter Thompson, I am of that breed of researcher turned planner. Invariably, those research craft skills gave me at least one leg to stand on when I transferred to the ad agency world.

When I became a department head, I learnt (to my cost) that there is no such thing as a junior planner, nor a trainee planner. (Of course there is, but until they have got a few years experience under their belt, they are more of a liability than an asset.) Having a research background means that I can devise survey methodologies, devise samples, moderate groups, write reports/debriefs, develop stimulus material, crunch numbers, design questionnaires, decipher data, understand econometric modelling and so on. These skills have enabled me, along with experience and deeper immersion on accounts over time, to be a great deal more authoritative on consumer understanding and consumer response to creative ideas. It may be currently 'uncool' to possess any research craft skills, to be completely phased by Millward Brown's Awareness Index, to be a focus group 'virgin', but people who can't or won't 'do' proper research are missing a terribly important trick. So I am with Stanley on that one.

THE TRUTH ABOUT ADVERTISING IS THAT IT WORKS IN LOTS OF DIFFERENT WAYS

What really gets me going on this subject is the pedalling of some sort of universal theory stated as fact by research companies with a nicely packaged, predetermined, streamlined methodology with lots of 'norms' to prove that one size fits all. All you have to do is decide if you are a 'recall' or 'persuasion' worshipper. And then they'll sell you some matching tracking study to tie in with their pre-testing product (which of course may or may not have anything whatsoever to do with the actual sales generated). Great for operational efficiency and profitability (of the research company), lousy for the creativity that could make a big difference to the brand in both the short and long term. It's not just silly, it's irresponsible.

> Advertisements are not a commodity product and their effects do not obey universal rules.
> (Simon Broadbent)

The job of advertising within the marketing mix is ultimately about sales but those sales come about in myriad different ways (and none of them are straightforward to measure).

[The word] 'sell' implies that you're after an immediate, directly linked transaction; yet a great deal of advertising is not. A great deal of advertising is maintaining brand relevance and brand value.
(Jeremy Bullmore)

Since there will very likely be ad effects over more than one year, agree your long-term objectives first. Take these into account, as well as the current year's goals, when you write ad objectives.
(Simon Broadbent)

Sadly, most American advertisers seem to believe that all advertising is like direct response advertising, simply there to generate short-term sales. (And most of their advertising pre-testing methodologies seem to emanate from direct marketing theory conceived in the 1920s by Claude Hopkins, Dr Daniel Starch and Dr George Gallup. Ancient theories still pertinent to DM, but not to all forms of brand communication I'm afraid.) Here in the UK, thanks in part to the efforts of Simon Broadbent and his IPA effectiveness awards which have been going since 1980, we now know that advertising does a great deal more than this. Advertising helps to build brands by maintaining or increasing brand values.

People value brands for who they are as much as what they do.... More and more do we find our rewards in life from the non-functional. These rewards tend to be more intense, more meaningful.
(Stephen King)

The defensive role of advertising is just as important. Sometimes we advertise and nothing positive happens, sales remain static. Does that mean the advertising didn't work? Not necessarily – it could have prevented sales from declining. Brand values can decay and need updating, advertising can do a very good (but unheroic) job of maintenance, helping a brand's sales stay where they are in the face of tough competition.

What both the recallers and the persuaders agree is that advertising can generate immediate sales predominantly by using new news around the rational benefits of the brand. All well and good, but in the majority of instances, advertising is not able to create this short-term effect. Not least because in these days of product parity, fewer brands possess meaningful, motivating points of difference they can boast about, and if they do, someone will copy them pretty soon anyway.

Similarly, if people remember your brand's advertising, and talk about it with others afterwards, that can be a good thing. But never forget that even the inventor of the AI admits that 'the Awareness Index is a measure of the opportunity to communicate, not a measure of sales effectiveness per se' (Gordon Brown, 1994). All it means is that you have created an ad people can remember; more importantly, you have created some currency or 'talkability' around the brand; it does not necessarily mean that when the ad goes out into the market place it will generate sales. Sadly, all too many clients in my experience fetishistically abuse this tool by using it as a traffic light to lean against (if you'll pardon the mixed metaphor).

Net net, advertising campaigns can have more than one objective, more than one target audience, more than one effect in the marketplace. We need to pay a great deal of attention at the brief writing phase to what the job is we are asking the advertising to do for the brand, and how we expect it to work (and how we are going to measure it).

MARKET RESEARCH IS IMPORTANT TO BRAND UNDERSTANDING BUT TECHNIQUES HAVE ALWAYS BEEN THEORETICALLY WEAK – BEWARE!

The points above and this one are inextricably linked. You can only decide what stimulus to use, whom to show it to, what methodology to use, what questions to ask, in which order and so on when you have agreed your theory of how your communication is going to work, how your consumer is going to respond to it. Moreover, it is highly unlikely the (pre-packaged) research tools you have at your disposal are going to fit your unique theory.

> If advertising works mainly by giving added values to a brand in the long run, what can we learn from a single exposure advertisement test whose results are based on short-term switching?
> (Stephen King)

Have we learnt nothing in the 30 years since he wrote that?

> Advertising, if it works at all, changes brand equity (memories) but not
> necessarily sales.... The idea that advertising performance should be
> judged by the changes in brand equity, not sales, is unpopular. We can
> measure sales well enough but measuring what we carry round between
> our ears is problematic.
> (Tim Ambler in Ambler and Vakratsas, 1998)

Apparently not. Stanley Pollitt, probably even now rotating 6 feet (2
metres?) under, when asked for his predictions on the future of advertising research back in 1969, observed:

> [I would guess that] there will be greater awareness of the complexity of
> the advertising process. This may mean that we will be less impatient to
> search for apparently simple numerical measurements of individual
> parts of it.... A simple fact which the numerate people who predominate
> in advertising research never seem to grasp, is that numbers to the innu-
> merate are seen as infallible. Liberally used as they have been in adver-
> tising research in the 1960s they have come to be associated with wrong
> and impractical findings, as such they are something of a God that has
> failed.

Sadly there are still FAR too many 'brand managers' believing that 'the
mere fact of getting some numbers constitutes an objective assessment of
the quality and effectiveness of the ad' (Hedges, 1974). Too many people
substituting a lack of understanding about advertising for a lack of understanding about a branded research technique. Too many junior brand
managers relying on the 'science and objectivity' of market research
results to make decisions beyond their remit. Too many researchers who
know lots about research but little about anything else, and clients who
bask confidently in the certainty that advertising works in one way only.

At the risk of repeating myself, advertising is far too complex for one
approach to be able to take it all in, let alone reduce it to one number.

There is also another perennial issue with the very nature of advertising
research – the process of data collection:

> Economists are not the only parties trying to impose rationality where it
> does not belong. Market Researchers, themselves rational people, look
> for logical explanations, and pseudo-solutions are sold to almost equally
> rational marketers. Consumers are asked to rationalize their decisions by

strangers with clipboards. The results are computer processed and reprocessed. Any true feelings that lay behind the buyer behaviour have been long lost by then.
(Tim Ambler in Ambler and Vakratsas, 1998)

All too many of those pre-packaged pre-testing techniques and off the shelf tracking modelling methodologies seem to be dependent on consumers giving a verbal post rationalization of events. Why is that? Just bear in mind that the mere act of asking someone to articulate something they have barely ever considered, let alone spoken out loud, is going to have an (editing) effect on what they say.

Which leads me on to 'safety in numbers' or the 'We couldn't measure A so we measured B instead' school of market research. As house prices, mortgages and school fees soar in direct correlation with job insecurity, so the 'mission to measure' has evolved.

If a possible effect is not measured (because to do so is too hard or too expensive) the absence of that measure does not mean the effect does not exist. Be careful: you are in danger of overlooking the effect, and it is wrong to do so just because you do not have a number.
(Simon Broadbent)

The definitive booklet on the uses and abuses of advertising research remains Alan Hedges' *Testing to Destruction*, first published in 1974 and reprinted by the IPA in a rather clever updated format with notes and commentary in 1997. In it, he makes four basic conclusions:

- It is not possible to make a realistic test of the effectiveness of a commercial in a laboratory situation in advance of real-life exposure.
- The most important contribution that research can make to increasing the selling effectiveness of advertising is at the planning stage before anyone has even begun to think about particular advertising ideas.
- Once work starts on specific advertising ideas the role of research is to provide a feedback from the consumer, enabling the creators and managers of advertising to learn about the properties of different ideas and approaches.
- Once the campaign is running, research can help to show how far objectives are being met and to redefine the objectives for the future.

Three of these points remain valid; point one can only be disallowed if you are solely interested in the short-term effects of conveying some 'new news' about the brand. The second point is a simple economic truth – sound consumer research and planning are considerably less wasteful than using creative time, energy and effort against the wrong brief. The magic word in the third paragraph for me is 'learn' – research does not make decisions, it demands interpretation and thought. The fourth point plays right back into Stephen King's Planning Cycle – not only to judge the effects of the campaign but to feed back learning as the cycle starts up again. I can't better this. If you haven't read this booklet, and advertising research is part of your life, do so now.

CONCLUSIONS

In this chapter I have tried to convey some of the passions and frustrations I feel about my chosen career in this fascinating and challenging world of brands and brand communications. One thing I do know is that it ain't ever going to be easy; it is intellectually demanding and you must never relax or drop your guard in the battle to get your brand a fair hearing in the big wide world. You can, however, take solace in the knowledge that far greater brains have been down this path before you, and left all sorts of useful hints and thoughts behind them that you can use to help illuminate the way. I just wish I had unearthed them a lot earlier.

REFERENCES AND FURTHER READING

Ambler, T and Vakratsas, D (1998) How to manage brand equity, *Market Leader*, 1

Broadbent, S (1992) 456 views of how advertising works, *Admap*, September/November

Broadbent, S (2001) Article, *Market Leader*, Autumn

Broadbent, T (1997) Pre-testing methods: the agony of choice, *Admap*, October

Brown, Gordon (Millward Brown) (1994) *Plumbing and Shirts*, Millward Brown Conference, March

Bullmore, J (1991) *Behind the Scenes in Advertising*, NTC

Bullmore, J (2001) *Posh Spice and Persil*, The Brands Lecture, December

Bullmore, J (2002) On the couch, *Campaign*, January

Damasio, A (1994) *Descartes' Error: Emotion, reason and the human brain*, London: Papermac (Macmillan)

FitzGerald, N (CEO, Unilever plc) (2001) *Life and Death of the World's Brands*, Annual Marketing Society Lecture

Gardner, B B and Levy, S J (1955) The product and the brand, *Harvard Business Review*, March–April

Hedges, A (1974) *Testing to Destruction*, IPA

King, S (1970) What is a brand? JWT Booklet

King, S (1977) *Developing New Brands*, Halstead Press

King, S (1978) Crisis in Branding, JWT Booklet, June

King, S (1991) Brand-building in the 1990s, *Journal of Marketing Management*

Klein, N (2001) *No Logo*, Flamingo

Lannon, J (1993) Branding essentials and the new environment, *Admap*, June

Lannon, J (1994) What brands need now, *Admap*, September

Pollitt, S (1979) How I started account planning in agencies, *Campaign*, April (reprinted in *Pollitt on Planning*, 2000)

Pollitt, S (1969) Learning from research in the 1960s, *Admap* (reprinted in *Pollitt on Planning*, 2000)

Index

NB: page numbers in italics indicate figures and tables